Giving It Some Thought

Cases for Early Childhood Practice

Muriel K. Rand

A 2000 NAEYC Comprehensive Membership Benefit

National Association for the Education of Young Children
Washington, D.C.

Photographs copyright © by

Marilyn Nolt/17, 67, 179
Jonathan A. Meyers/23
Linda Werstiuk/29
Tom Mcguire/34
Denise Hogan/42
Jean-Claude LeJeune/47, 52, 79,
    83, 106, 126, 131, 140, 152
Nancy P. Alexander/57, 157
Michael Siluk/73, 172
Cleo Photography/92
Cris M. Kelly/98
Renaud Thomas/101, 142
Elaine M. Ward/108
Jeffrey High/115
Kathy Sloan/121

Marietta Lynch/149
Photo Marketing Unlimited/154
Ellen Galinsky/164

Front cover, clockwise from upper left:
Bettina Bairly
Cleo photography
Renaud Thomas
Francis Wardle
BmPorter/Don Franklin
BmPorter/Don Franklin

Back cover, left to right:
Bill Geiger
BmPorter/Don Franklin
BmPorter/Don Franklin
Bill Geiger

National Association for the Education of Young Children
1509 16th Street, NW
Washington, DC 20036-1426
202-232-8777 or 800-424-2460
www.naeyc.org

Through its publications program the National Association for the Education of Young Children (NAEYC) provides a forum for discussion of major issues and ideas in the early childhood field, with the hope of provoking thought and promoting professional growth. The views expressed or implied are not necessarily those of the Association. NAEYC thanks the author, who donated much time and effort to develop this book as a contribution to the profession.

Library of Congress Catalog Card Number: 00-102450
ISBN 0-935989-94-3
NAEYC #150

Publications editor: Carol Copple
Production manager: Jack Zibulsky
Copyediting: Catherine Cauman
Editorial assistance: Debra Beland and Lacy Thompson
Cover and book design and production: Malini Dominey

Printed in the United States of America

About the Author

Muriel K. Rand, Ed.D., is the assistant dean of the College of Education at New Jersey City University. Since beginning her career as a preschool teacher, Dr. Rand has spent the last 15 years working with preservice and inservice teachers as a curriculum developer, mentor teacher, college professor, and consultant to child care centers and public school districts. Her interest in advocacy and social policy has lead to leadership positions in the New Jersey Professional Development Center for Early Care and Education, the New Jersey Early Care and Education Coalition, the New Jersey Association for the Education of Young Children, and the New Jersey Association of Early Childhood Teacher Educators. Dr. Rand has published articles and book chapters on case-based pedagogy, early literacy, and early childhood teacher education. She has also coauthored a casebook for student teachers, *Voices of Student Teachers: Cases from the Field*, published by Merrill in 1999.

Contents

Preface

Questions, questions, questions. What do I do about Ellen's biting? How can I get my director to understand developmentally appropriate practice? How can we move away from standardized testing? What is the best way to teach my children tolerance?

Early childhood educators may find their work demanding and rewarding, confusing and enlightening, complex and humbling. The challenges of working with young children and the windows of opportunity to influence children's learning and development make the field of early childhood education unique. Decisions, major and minor, made by adults working with young children constitute a primary factor in the quality of children's early care and education. Stated simply, teachers make a great difference in the lives of young children.

There is a growing crisis in the quality of early childhood programs today, fueled partly by the lack of well-trained, knowledgeable, reflective teachers (Cryer & Phillipsen 1997; Kagan & Neuman 1997). Teachers need more professional development opportunities and tools to help them strengthen their understanding of young children's needs, improve their relationships with families and community, and support their role in creating quality care and education.

This volume presents teaching cases that reflect typical challenges in teaching. A valuable tool for professional development, the cases provide a basis for discussing teacher decisions and actions, thereby developing problem-solving abilities, decisionmaking skills, and powers of reflection. This process allows new teachers to build a repertoire of "experiences" that they have thought deeply about, and it helps experienced teachers to rethink situations and explore more profound issues in teaching, including the ethics involved in making decisions (Schön 1987).

Forty-nine actual cases bring to life many of the emotions, issues, and concerns of early childhood educators. They cover the spectrum of center-based early childhood settings—Head Start, nursery schools, private child care centers, kindergartens, and preschool and primary programs in public schools—and a variety of cultural contexts found in urban, suburban, and rural locales.

The book touches on numerous issues in early childhood, with the cases grouped in seven larger sections addressing the challenges of working with parents, curriculum, classroom communities, children with special needs, stress in children's lives, antibias practices, and workplace settings. Each section represents age levels from infants/toddlers through second grade. The open-ended nature of the cases makes this book useful in a variety of professional development settings: undergraduate and graduate-level college courses, CDA training programs, inservice workshops, staff meetings.

Giving It Some Thought provides a way for those working with young children or preparing to work with young children to think deeply about their own decisionmaking and grow in their ability to be reflective. Using case discussions promotes active, learner-centered instruction and can help teachers take responsibility for their own professional growth.

Cryer, D., & L. Phillipsen. 1997. Quality details: A close-up look at child care program strengths and weaknesses. *Young Children* 52 (5): 51–61.

Kagan, S.L., & M.J. Neuman. 1997. Highlights of the Quality 2000 Initiative: Not by chance. *Young Children* 52 (6): 54–62.

Schön, D. 1987. *Educating the reflective practitioner*. San Francisco: Jossey-Bass.

Acknowledgments

Giving It Some Thought is the result of listening to many fascinating voices from the early childhood community. I deeply thank the following people, who were kind enough to share their experiences and ideas with me:

Teresa Barroqueira
Lyn Berardinelli
Cindy Bodnar
Alicia Carasquilla
Doug Castner
Cheryl Devine
Tracey Lynn Dunn
Jody Eberly
Betsy Geiger
Lori Grabowski
Chris Hills
Paula Johnson
Lori Ann Kyak
Sandra Lima
Crystal Lofton

Pam Mancini
Basiliki Manolis
Joy Menzel
Briana Nurse
Jennifer Orzepowski
Sister Alice Ottapurackal
Christine Pawlikoski
Michelle Raimondo
John Rand
Meg Rothberg
Melissa Salmon
Kristy Schaub
Rosemary Tavarez
Harriet Worobey
Amy Yee.

This book is dedicated to
Cheryl Devine and Harriet Worobey,
who provided the opportunities for my own children
to discover the joy of learning, and who set them
on successful paths in life.

Introduction

Why Use Cases?
How Do We Start?

Ⓗow often have we sat together during breaks, over lunch, or at the end of the day sharing stories about the children and our work? Teachers love stories almost as much as children do. Although we may not have a formal time set aside to reflect on our teaching, we still share with one another our problems and successes, hopes and dreams, needs and frustrations.

This book communicates the ideas and experiences of early childhood teachers through teaching cases—personal narratives that focus on significant challenges in teaching practices, relationships, and decisionmaking. The narratives fall into the "cases" category because they represent larger ideas that are worthy of reflection and deliberation (Miller & Kantrov 1998).

A tool to help improve teaching

Cases can help us think differently about our teaching, react to problems in new ways, and see possibilities different from those we have seen before. Cases allow teachers to think and talk about problems, issues, and concerns outside the immediate work setting. We have the opportunity to step back and reflect without the demands of the busy classroom. It is difficult when making many decisions every minute in our classrooms to think deeply about what is happening and analyze our decisions. Examining and discussing cases gives us the time and objectivity to think about what we have done well or could do differently.

Examining cases also allows us to develop a fuller repertoire of experiences upon which to draw when making decisions. We can "experience" events and react to them, discussing different viewpoints and possible actions. When similar circumstances occur in our classrooms, we then can make decisions based on thoughtful reflection rather than spontaneous reaction. This clearly is valuable for the new teacher with limited experience, but it is helpful also for the veteran teacher whose reactions may be somewhat automatic.

Discussing and analyzing cases makes us think about *why* we are making the decisions we make. Using cases is especially effective in staff development sessions, workshops, and college courses because these settings bring together teachers with very different backgrounds and breadths of teaching experience. By listening to others' viewpoints, debating, and articulating our ideas, we clarify our understandings about teaching.

Most of us enjoy reading about other teachers' experiences and thinking about what we might do in the same situation. The cases in this book are interesting and motivating. They are open ended, depicting a dilemma facing a teacher, with no outcome given so that readers can determine for themselves what they would do. The lack of resolution may be unsettling at first, but it provides the opportunity for exciting discussions and creative thinking. Finally, as we struggle to make sense of teaching cases, sharing our own experiences and understandings, a community of learners evolves, creating a support system for all involved.

Using cases to dig deeper into issues in early childhood teaching allows us to be active in our own professional development. Just as children do not learn best by passively receiving information, neither do adults. Case discussions allow a partnership between "learners" and "teachers" to develop so that the lines between teaching and learning become blurred. In early childhood education as well as in adult professional development, "not all the teaching should be done by the teacher. Not all the learning should be done by the students" (Gragg 1994, 15).

Getting started:
Methods for analyzing the cases

The cases in this book are broadly grouped according to their main focus. All the cases are complex and deal with a range of issues. There is no set order in which to read or use the cases, so you may find yourself jumping from one case to another, one section to another.

There is never one right answer when analyzing what action a teacher should take. Because teaching is complex and many variables affect what goes on in a program, isolating one particular action is often impossible. The best way to approach these cases is to brainstorm many different possibilities and predict the outcome for each. It is helpful then to carefully think about the relevant factors in making a decision about what to do.

This is an opportune time to go back to the reading you have done on early childhood education issues or to look for new reading material to help clarify the decisions the teacher could make. Analyzing cases can often help you put the abstract ideas in books into a practical, understandable framework. (A listing of pertinent readings is found at the end of each of the seven sections of the book.)

The analysis of a case also depends on whether you're looking for an immediate solution to be carried out quickly, planning for a long-term solution, or brainstroming ideas for preventing the occurrence of a particular situation in the first place. All of these possibilities can be explored, especially during group discussions and sharing. It is often eye-opening to discover that others read a case very differently from you and come up with solutions you might never have considered.

Group discussions are most productive when analysis and participation are structured according to the needs and expectations of the group rather than being left unstructured. The methods outlined on the pages that follow can be adapted to fit the different needs of different groups, be they workshop attendees, inservice training participants, or students in a college or graduate-level seminar.

Identifying-the-problems method. This method involves two steps: first identifying the causes of the problems in the case and next identifying solutions based on those causes.

The selected case is read before the group meets, and then the case is read aloud again during the meeting to refresh everyone's memory. Although reading aloud takes time, many people find it enjoyable and it brings the case into focus. Next, the group briefly reviews the main characters, the setting, and the episodes of the case.

Participants then break into discussion groups in which they are asked only to identify the problems in the case and what may be causing them. Solutions are not yet discussed because at this point they would distract group members from delving deeper into the causes of the problems. Referring to books or other reading material can help group members focus their ideas.

The entire group next gathers again to share the problems and causes they have identified.

After the larger group has shared ideas, the small groups reconvene to discuss possible solutions on *two levels:* short-term (immediate) solutions and long-term solutions. The whole group then gathers one final time to share these solutions.

The emphasis during this process is always on thinking through many possibilities, not pinpointing one right answer. Problems and solutions can be related to readings that synthesize theories and research in early childhood education.

Writing-response method. Participants are paired as writing partners and each pair is assigned a case to read before meeting together. Each partner is free to write a response about any aspect of the case that he considers important. Partners take copies of their responses to exchange with each other at meeting time.

When they meet, participants first break into pairs and discuss either open-ended questions such as those at the end of the cases in this book or questions that they themselves generate.

The whole group then gathers to share responses.

Before the class meets again, each participant reads his partner's written response and writes a new reply to give to his partner about how his own ideas may have changed.

Case-switching method. Groups of participants are assigned (or self-select) to read one case, while other groups read different cases. After using either of the two methods of analysis just described, one group restates the case, explains the main issues, and shares the responses with a group that has not read the case. Groups then switch roles.

One value in this method is the challenge of understanding a case well enough to explain it to others who have not read it. This helps members go below the surface as they reconstruct the events of the case.

Open-ended-issues method. Participants read the case before meeting and may also be asked to respond in writing. They then meet together as a whole group or in small groups and brainstorm all the possible issues. This may take more time than expected since at first one tends to see cases as black and white when they really are more complex. With a lot of encouragement, the group moves beyond first impressions.

When the group has generated a list of pertinent issues, it can identify theories, research, future topics, or readings to address each issue. Readings can be assigned to clarify the relevance of course work or theory to classroom experiences.

Perspective-taking method. The perspective that we take while reading a case affects how we perceive the issues. Cases can be read aloud or enacted in informal role play with group members taking on the parts of characters in the cases.

After the enactment, participants keep their roles to debate the issues of the case, articulating their characters' thoughts and feelings. Participants must be willing to suspend their own beliefs while they role-play. Other group members can take sides in the debate and ask questions of the characters to help them explain their views. This method provides new insight into the feelings of the characters and helps us see the complexity of many issues.

Engaging participants in case discussions

What happens when discussions are dominated by one or two people? How do we get the group members who are quiet and reserved to share their ideas? How do we ensure that everyone actively and enthusiastically participates and no ideas are squelched? Some useful techniques to help balance the participation and create a positive climate for case discussion are shared here.

Whether case analyses are used in college classes, staff meetings, inservice workshops, or training courses, the most critical aspect of case discussions is building an environment of trust. Participants need to feel confidence in risking their self-esteem to put forth new ideas. A comfortable, nonthreatening environment helps draw as many participants as possible into actively contributing to discussions.

Active listening

One way to help learners feel confident in expressing themselves is to have them work on active listening skills. Active listening means not just listening carefully to a speaker, but also being able to paraphrase or reflect back what the speaker said. We tend to focus our thoughts on our own ideas, often formulating our responses even before the speaker has finished. We may have our own agenda and not really listen carefully.

Active listening takes practice. It is worth spending the time required to master the skill, however, because it is as valuable for understanding young children as it is for understanding adults.

When we are truly heard, we feel validated and can consider feedback more productively. As a result, more ideas are generated and more learning takes place. Listening can foster among a group a sense of community that improves motivation, morale, and receptiveness to new ideas.

Communication Engendered by Active Listening

Kindergartner and Adult

Dialogue 1

Matthew (playing in the block area): Miss Liliana, Stevie pushed me!

Miss Liliana: He pushed you? What did you do to him?

Matthew: I didn't do anything to him, he just pushed me!

Miss Liliana: Well, he wouldn't have pushed you just for nothing! I'm tired of you two fighting. You're both going to have to find a different area to play in, right now! No more blocks today.

Dialogue 2

Matthew (playing in the block area): Miss Liliana, Stevie pushed me!

Miss Liliana: Oh! You're upset because Stevie pushed you?

Matthew: Yeah, he shoved me out of the way when I went to get a block.

Miss Liliana: So you were getting a block when Stevie pushed you.

Matthew: I couldn't reach the block I wanted, and I bumped into his block tower.

Miss Liliana: I guess you couldn't fit between the block tower and the cabinet.

Matthew: No! I'm gonna tell Stevie to move his block tower so it doesn't get knocked over!

Miss Liliana: Maybe we could put a mark on the rug to show where to leave space for kids to get to the block cabinet.

Matthew: Okay, I'll go get some tape to mark the rug!

To understand the difference between responses that reflect active listening and responses that shut down communication, read or enact the dialogues in the box "Communication Engendered by Active Listening." Notice that some comments seem to help the child and the adult, or the two adults, communicate and problem solve and other comments do not.

These dialogues show how easily a listener can open or close communication by her responses. Communication can be shut down by negative responses, unsolicited advice, or attempts to solve someone's problem for him. Most speakers want most of all to know that the audience has understood their point. That means not that listeners

Teacher and Center Director

Dialogue 1

Barbara (3-year-old-group teacher): I am so tired of having to clean up all the glue that gets on the art tables!

Lakeisha (director): That's part of your job, Barbara.

Barbara: But it's such a mess when I come in, I spend 15 minutes getting the tables ready for lunch, and then the kids are all waiting for my help in the bathroom.

Lakeisha: Why don't you talk to the other teachers in the room and see if you can figure out a way to clean up the glue more easily?

Barbara: They won't listen to me!

Lakeisha: Well, do you want me to talk to them?

Barbara: No, that won't work! Never mind, I'll figure it out myself.

Dialogue 2

Barbara (3-year-old-group teacher): I am so tired of having to clean up all the glue that gets on the art tables!

Lakeisha (director): It's taking you a long time to get the glue off?

Barbara: It is such a mess when I come in, I spend 15 minutes getting the tables ready for lunch, and then the kids are all waiting for my help in the bathroom.

Lakeisha: So the glue is already on the tables when you come in?

Barbara: Yeah, the other teachers never put newspapers down when the kids use glue.

Lakeisha: It sounds like the teachers forget to cover the tables when they set up.

Barbara: Well, I couldn't find any newspaper in the room. Can you get us some more?

Lakeisha: Sure, I'll bring it in first thing tomorrow morning.

Barbara: Thanks. Maybe I'll put up a sign reminding them to cover the tables.

Lakeisha: Let me know if that works!

necssarily *agree* with the speaker, but that listeners *hear* the speaker's ideas. It is comforting to know that others will not immediately shoot down our ideas but will truly consider them. This knowledge validates us as individuals, helps us to think more deeply, and empowers us to express our more creative ideas.

Another barrier to group sharing is negative nonverbal communication. We all know what it's like to have group members pass judgment through rolling eyes or folded arms or by turning away from the speaker. Letting the speaker know you are listening through nods, monosyllables ("Hmmm"), and body language is an important part of active listening, whether attending to adults or children.

Case discussions provide opportunities to practice listening techniques that we can use in our teaching. For more information about the power of active listening, check the suggestions for further reading at the end of this introduction.

Brainstorming

In many group meetings we allot time for brainstorming and value this process as a way of unearthing and sharing good ideas. In practice, however, brainstorming often falls short, with the group spending a great deal of time stuck on one persistent idea or shooting down other ideas before they get a chance to fly.

For brainstorming to be effective in helping us truly gain insight or in pushing ourselves to find new, creative solutions, two important steps need to be taken. First, it is essential that *all* ideas be accepted, no matter how crazy, off the topic, or absurd they seem. It is often the ridiculous idea that gets the creative impulses flowing and leads to innovative mental connections that would not have surfaced otherwise. In brainstorming, therefore, no one should be allowed to discuss the merits of an idea when it is first introduced.

Not launching into a discussion is tricky in group dynamics because we all want to voice our opinions on the ideas right away. It is critical that the group facilitator remind the participants often that ideas are being gathered, not evaluated.

The group eventually reaches a point where the flow of ideas decreases to a trickle or stops. When no more ideas can be generated, then the second step, evaluation, begins.

Evaluation is the time for speakers to defend their ideas and for others to ask questions and offer alternative perspectives. If the evaluation phase occurs too soon in the brainstorming process, the group comes to a dead end or wastes time and does not get very far. Because group members can become very intense about and committed to their own ideas, the evaluation phase is a good time to practice active listening and to use some process techniques discussed below.

Cooperative learning

Many ideas in the cooperative learning literature are successful with adults as well as children because they provide structure that ensures the more equal participation and active involvement of the whole group (Kagan 1994).

Round-robin. One simple way to ensure that all participants get a chance to contribute ideas is to use a round-robin technique. Participants first read through the case carefully. Next, they break into small groups and brainstorm the possible causes of the problem at hand or the issues involved in the case. During brainstorming, a sheet of paper is passed around in each small group and everyone writes down an idea until all ideas are exhausted. While one person is writing her idea on the round-robin sheet, others may jot down notes about their reactions to the case.

This activity can be repeated when groups discuss possible solutions to the problems.

Jigsaw. Another technique that requires everyone's active participation is the jigsaw technique. Participants are each assigned to two different types of groups, expert group and home group. Participants number off one to four, with each set of participants numbered one to four comprising a different home group, while all the ones comprise one expert group, the twos another, and so on. (There will be four expert groups, but the number of home groups depends on the number of participants in the whole group.)

First, the four expert groups meet, each thoroughly discussing one aspect of the case as assigned by the session leader or determined in advance by the whole group. Next, members form their home groups to put the issues into perspective and share the ideas from their various expert groups. The whole group then comes together to discuss the major outcomes.

Value lines. When participants need to get up and move around a bit, a value line provides an opportunity to stretch and a way to discuss issues more informally.

After reading a case, the whole group forms a line across the room, with one end representing an extreme position (such as "the teacher in the case was wrong" or "children should not be rewarded") and the other end representing the opposite extreme. Participants place themselves on the continuum between those extremes by talking to others next to them and deciding on which side they belong. Eventually everyone will be lined up in roughly the order of how they feel about the issue.

Conclusion

The popularity of using teaching cases in education continues to grow as we realize that this method can provide a link between academic preparation and classroom teaching. Case discussions help us use a model of active learning with adults that also establishes a community of learners in which new understandings are constructed by all participants.

A list of valuable books and articles on using cases for professional development follows, as well as the references for text citations.

References and resources for further reading

Bredekamp, S., & C. Copple, eds. 1997. *Developmentally appropriate practice in early childhood programs, revised edition.* Washington, DC: NAEYC.

This is the definitive source for information on the principles of developmentally appropriate practice for children, from birth through age 8, and on guidelines for making decisions in the classroom based on research and theory.

Colbert, J., K. Trimble, & P. Desberg, eds. 1996. *The case for education: Contemporary approaches for using case methods.* Boston: Allyn & Bacon.

Leaders in the field of case pedagogy share their honest stories of successes and failures in using cases in their classes with student teachers and in staff development programs.

Derber, C. 1979. *The pursuit of attention: Power and individualism in everyday life.* New York: Oxford University Press.

This small book goes beyond most treatments of active listening by illustrating how gender, class, and other social divisions profoundly affect who gets heard and who does not. Awareness of how attention is distributed in society can help sharpen listening skills.

Faber, A., & E. Mazlish. 1995. *How to talk so kids can learn at home and in school.* New York: Rawson Associates.

Illustrated with cartoon vignettes, this very readable book covers the use of active listening to deal with students' feelings that interfere with learning. Other topics include skills to get kids to cooperate, pitfalls of punishment, solving students' problems together, effective praise, how to free a child who is locked in a role, and the parent-teacher relationship.

Gordon, T. 1974. *TET: Teacher effectiveness training.* New York: Peter H. Wyden.

This classic volume has invaluable information on the teacher-learner relationship, avoiding roadblocks to communication, guidelines and uses for active listening, handling students' problems, preventing problems, and resolving conflicts.

Gragg, C.I. 1994. Teachers also must learn. In *Teaching and the case method: Text, cases, and readings,* 3d ed., eds. L.B. Barnes, C.R. Christensen, & A.J. Hansen, 15–22. Boston: Harvard Business School Press.

An overview of case-based teaching developed at Harvard's Business School is presented in this revised edition of the original classic. In addition to this chapter, the book includes many that focus on the practical aspects of leading case discussions.

Jones, E. 1986. *Teaching adults: An active learning approach*. Washington, DC: NAEYC.

This story of Jones's teaching journey is a call to action to both colleagues and students for more constructivist teaching, and it is an inspiration to those struggling against traditional lecture-course expectations.

Kagan, S. 1994. *Cooperative learning*. San Clemente, CA: Kagan Cooperative Learning.

A very practical guide to cooperative learning theory, methods, and lesson designs, and a thorough resource for applying cooperative learning to all ages, from kindergartner through adult.

Miller, B., & I. Kantrov. 1998. *A guide to facilitating cases in education*. Portsmouth, NH: Heinemann.

The authors point out that the value in using teaching cases lies in the discussion that it generates. They provide practical advice for guiding such discussions in a variety of group settings.

Rogers, K.R., & R.E. Farson. 1987. Active listening. In *Teaching and the case method*, ed. C. Roland Christensen. Boston: Harvard Business School Press.

Appearing in the case book developed at Harvard University's School of Business, this essay provides information on what active listening is, how to listen actively, and what to avoid.

Schön, D. 1987. *Educating the reflective practitioner*. San Francisco: Jossey-Bass.

A thorough volume on how to improve professional development in education to meet the needs of the complex, unpredictable problems of actual teaching practice by promoting reflection-in-action.

Schulman, J., ed. 1992. *Case methods in teacher education*. New York: Teachers College Press.

This edited volume has chapters covering all aspects of cases as teaching tools, cases as learning tools, prospects and limitations.

Wasserman, S. 1994. *Introduction to case method teaching: A guide to the galaxy*. New York: Teachers College Press.

An invaluable resource that covers teaching with cases, writing your own cases, preparing to teach, evaluation, and other helpful topics.

1

Challenges of Working with Parents

The Biter

Lena teaches a toddler class in which the parents are very upset about a child's repeated biting. How can Lena help Ellen, who is almost 2, stop biting and also help the parents who are worried about their own children?

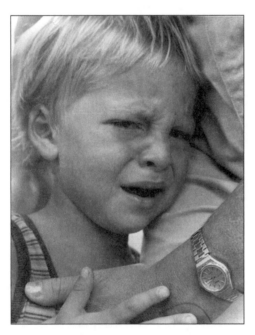

As I hug Jessica, applying ice to the red mark on her arm, I can't help feeling frustrated by the problems that Ellen is creating with her repeated biting.

It's October in our toddler room. Our 16 youngsters range in age from just turning 2 to young 3s. Our room is small but well equipped; I like to think of it as cozy.

I've worked at the center for 15 years, most of the time with the toddlers. Gretchen, one of the assistant teachers, has been here even longer. I think we've lost count of how many years she's helped in our toddler room. Latoya, our other assistant, just started over the summer. She's young and enthusiastic and has brought a lot of energy into our classroom.

I love the joys and challenges of this age group. One of the inevitable difficulties, however, seems to be biting. Almost every year we have a child who occasionally tries out a bite or two. This year Ellen has presented us with this challenge, only it seems a bit worse than those I've dealt with before.

Ellen is not quite 2 yet. She is inquisitive, curious, and full of energy (like most 2-year-olds I guess!). She seems fascinated with the other children and spends a lot of time watching them and following them around. Every so often she just leans over and bites—a leg, an arm, whatever intrigues her at the moment. Of course she gets a huge reaction from this, which interests her even more!

I think that Ellen's biting is part of her need to explore her world. Babies learn right after birth to explore their environments with their mouths. It seems reasonable to me that Ellen still has this pattern of behavior and is exploring what happens when she bites, and the reactions she gets have added to the allure. We sternly let her know that biting is not acceptable, and we try to give our attention to the victim rather than to Ellen.

We have spoken to Ellen's parents about her biting. They of course are horrified. I've tried to let them know that it's a natural part of her learning and exploration and that it will soon stop, but they are clearly upset. Every afternoon they approach me apprehensively and ask, "How was Ellen today?" They have tried hard to get Ellen to stop biting, but the behavior continues. I've been through this with other children, and I really do have confidence that Ellen will learn and that the behavior will decrease and then end.

Meanwhile the other parents in the toddler room are going crazy over this. I've tried to protect Ellen's privacy, but the parents gossip and they know who's doing the biting. Some tell their children to stay away from Ellen, some have complained to the director. I explain calmly that we too are very concerned and are dealing with the problem. I also explain to parents that some behaviors are an inevitable part of group care. We've even had parents from other classrooms ask their teachers about the biting and what's being done about it. I'm not sure why they're worried when it's not in their children's classes.

Last night I attended a meeting of the Parent Advisory Committee. When we got to new business, one of the parents from my class brought up the biting problem. "Would it be possible to put something in the newsletter?" Mrs. Weng asked. "Perhaps you could ask parents to explain to their children that biting is not allowed at school."

I was very surprised. How could parents think that the biting would end if a parent just "explained" to his child that biting was bad? Don't they realize what the parents of the biter are going through? Or how hard they are working to get her to stop? Or the stress that they are under? I can understand how upsetting it must be to have your child bitten at school; however, some of these parents are really blowing the problem out of proportion, aren't they?

Discussion questions

1. What do you think about the way Lena is handling the challenge of getting Ellen to stop biting? Can you think of a different approach that might be more successful or other ideas that Lena could try? What health and safety concerns, especially regarding communicable diseases, need to be considered?

2. How would you reply to Mrs. Weng? What would you say to the parents in this class?

3. What do you think the role of the director should be in talking with parents about the biting problem?

4. Why do you think Ellen is biting? Do you think Lena is right? What do you know about this age that would help you understand Ellen? How can Jean Piaget's developmental theory help us understand? How about Lawrence Kohlberg's theory of moral development? Erik Erikson's stages of psychosocial development?

5. Retell this case from the perspective of one of the toddlers' parents. Now tell it from Ellen's parents' standpoint. What can you learn from viewing the situation through their eyes?

Toilet Training:
Ready or Not!

Janeen is struggling with the demands of parents who want their son Bharat to use the toilet. She feels that 2½-year-old Bharat is simply not ready and that it is inappropriate and frustrating to continue to push him. Whose decision should this be?

I teach at a small suburban child care center in which we believe that we are here to serve the parents' needs. We go out of our way to be open to parents' suggestions, needs, and help. We have a liberal open-door policy and invite parents to share their talents, skills, and customs with the children. Our board of trustees is made up of parents, and we are deeply committed to the philosophy of parents and teachers working in collaboration. Our parents are predominantly professionals from a variety of cultures, many Asian. I am the teacher of our toddlers, 12 children in all, ages 2 and 3.

My problem stems from one little boy, Bharat, who is 28 months old this week. He has shown no interest in using the toilet. In our program this is acceptable because toileting is viewed as a natural developmental skill that will come in time. However, Bharat's parents have made it clear to me that they want him trained, no matter what!

Last week at pickup time, we had another conversation like many before. Mrs. Shah asked me how Bharat had done that day using the toilet.

I stated calmly, "Bharat doesn't show developmental signs of being ready to use the toilet yet."

Mrs. Shah answered, "How could he not be ready? All of the other children in our family and our neighborhood used the toilet long before Bharat's age. In our country it is expected that children will be toilet trained by now."

I tried again to convince her, saying, "Pushing Bharat might be traumatic for him in the long run."

Mrs. Shah replied, "Bharat uses the toilet when he is at home. We regularly bring him to the bathroom and he is successful. We think he's just lazy and that's why he won't do it at school. He needs to have more pressure put on him to try."

I meekly replied that we would try our best to work with Bharat.

Well, during the day at school, Bharat never asks to go, he shows no interest in the toilet when we are in the bathroom, and if we mention using the potty he begins to fuss loudly. He goes into a full kicking, screaming, crying tantrum every time we firmly insist. To get him on the toilet, he has to be held down. This just breaks my heart, and I know it is the wrong thing to do. We are causing him stress, and I worry that the trauma will affect him later in life.

This is not the first time this has happened in my 15 years of teaching. I regularly work with parents to help them understand the process young children go through in learning to use the toilet. I don't have children of my own, so understanding the parents' views is sometimes difficult for me. It seems to become a competition for some parents when other children are using the toilet before their child. They also worry, I'm sure, that something might be wrong with their child if he or she is not using the toilet by a certain age.

Our school's policy on toilet training backs me up completely, but I am the one who faces the daily problems of talking to parents and working with the children. Mrs. Shah asked me this morning to meet again at pickup time to discuss Bharat's progress. I just don't know what to do. How can I force a child to use the toilet when I know it is not appropriate and may hurt him psychologically? But can I just go against parents' needs and desires?

Discussion questions

1. Why do you think Janeen is not comfortable in forcing Bharat to use the toilet? What do you know about child development that supports Janeen's views?

2. Why do you think Bharat's parents are so insistent? Retell this case from their perspective. What have you learned from looking at the situation through their eyes?

3. What role do cultural differences play in this issue? Are there different expectations for children's development based on cultural norms? What other areas of development are culturally based?

4. Think about this case from Bharat's perspective. What do you think he is feeling? What do you think his understanding of using the toilet is? Why do you think he resists using the toilet?

5. What would you do in Janeen's place? Brainstorm as many possible solutions as you can.

"I Told Him to Hit Back"

Miss Jacobs is working hard to teach Mario, one of her kindergartners, to use words rather than hitting to solve problems. She is surprised when Mario's mother tells her she teaches him to hit back so he doesn't get bullied and can learn to survive in the "real world."

"Mario! Use your words! You may not hit Carlos. Tell him you don't like that!"

I feel as though I've said those words a hundred times. In fact I think I *have* said those words a hundred times, and they don't seem to do much good. Mario is a sweet little kindergartner, but he hasn't learned to handle his frustration without pushing or hitting. He rarely ever starts a problem. He's rather quiet and tends to work and play by himself. But if anyone confronts him or any conflicts develop, he uses action first to solve the problem.

For example, yesterday Mario was working in the block area. He spent a lot of time creating an incredibly complex building, which he told me was a hospital. I can tell he's very strong in his representational ability. As Mario was putting on the final touches, Hector decided he needed a block from the top of Mario's building.

Mario screamed, "Give that back to me!" as he grabbed the block out of Hector's hand and pushed him hard, sending Hector tumbling backward onto the floor. Hector started crying in indignation, and Mario returned calmly to his building.

I checked to make sure Hector was okay, and I gave him sympathy while I gently brought both boys together to talk about the incident. I began by saying, "Hector, you can't just grab a block from someone else's building. You should have asked Mario before you took it."

"But it's the only one like that. Me and Joseph needed it for our castle. Mario hogs all the blocks."

"I do not!" shouted Mario.

I said calmly to Mario, "If someone bothers you, use your words and tell him that you're upset. I can't let you grab and push. That's not how we solve our problems in school. Now if Hector bothers you, what should you do?"

"Well, my mom says if someone bothers me I should stick up for myself. Like if someone hits me, I should hit him back."

"Mario, we can't have hitting in school. I'll talk to your mother and explain it to her. I'm sure she'll agree with me. Now both of you boys say you're sorry and then go back to the block center."

Both mumbled a barely audible "I'm sorry," then headed back to the block area.

During lunch I made a quick call to Hector's mother, asking if I could meet with her for a few minutes after school. She agreed.

Our school is in a working-class Hispanic neighborhood in a small city. Many of the children are Dominican, some are Cuban, and the rest are Puerto Rican. Most live in tough neighborhoods where gangs are prevalent and drug use is all over the place. I'm sure the parents work hard to protect their kids from the bad influences.

I grew up in a rural area south of here and have taught at this school for about three years now. It's taken me a long time to get used to the city environment and the Hispanic culture of the children, but I feel like I've learned a lot and come a long way.

After school Mario stayed in the classroom with our assistant teacher while I led Mrs. Ortiz to an empty room next door. "Thank you so much for coming, Mrs. Ortiz. I appreciate it. Mario is doing very well academically in school. I can tell he's a very bright boy. That's why I need your advice."

I could see Mrs. Ortiz's shoulders relax a bit. "How can I help you?" she asked.

"Well, Mario never starts any problems, but often when someone bothers him, he reacts by hitting or pushing. I'm trying to get him to talk out solutions, to use his words to let the other children know how he feels. He's told me that you encourage him to hit back."

"Well, Miss Jacobs, words are just fine, but I think you're being unrealistic. Do you have any idea what kind of neighborhood we live in? I have to prepare Mario for surviving in that world. He needs to know how to stand up for himself. Words don't solve problems on the streets. Mario needs to be able to defend himself. Yes, I've taught him that if someone hits him, he better hit back. Otherwise he's going to end up getting picked on by the bullies!"

I stared at Mrs. Ortiz in quiet disbelief. On the surface her reasoning sounded logical, but how could I condone violent solutions to problems? I believe that is one of the reasons we have so many problems with gangs and violence to begin with.

What could I say to Mrs. Ortiz? How could we reach a solution?

Discussion questions

1. Whose philosophy comes closer to your own, Miss Jacobs's or Mrs. Ortiz's?

2. Do you think it is possible to have a different standard of behavior in the classroom from that at home? Will children adapt to a double standard, or will they be confused? What evidence from your own experiences as a child can you give to support your reasoning?

3. Using Lawrence Kohlberg's views of how children develop moral reasoning, justify Miss Jacobs's attempts to have Mario use words instead of actions.

4. Retell this case from Mrs. Ortiz's standpoint. From this perspective, what have you learned that could help Miss Jacobs?

5. When parents and teachers have differences in philosophy and practice, what is the best way to proceed while keeping the child's best interest at heart? Should both sides compromise? Should one adult give in? Should the parent try to find a different school (which may not be possible)? What advice can you give Miss Jacobs and Mrs. Ortiz?

Are You Getting My
Child Ready?

Gail is surprised at back-to-school night when she explains her developmentally appropriate curriculum for 3-year-olds and some parents still show concern about getting their child ready for formal academic instruction.

This is my first year teaching, and I am lucky to have found a child care center that is nationally accredited and has a child-centered philosophy that I agree with. I am in charge of a class of eighteen 3-year-olds. Most of the children are African American like me and have parents in professional jobs in our local suburbs, which border a large city. There is a good deal of competition among child care centers in the area, and we have a substantial waiting list. I work in a team with two assistant teachers who have helped build my confidence. I feel well prepared after my many field experiences and my college education courses.

I started working in June as the class gradually and smoothly made the transition from the toddler room over the summer months. Now it is the end of September and I'm comfortable and pleased with the way the class is running and how much the kids are learning. I thought everything was going well for my first year—that is, until back-to-school night.

I was a bit nervous about leading my first back-to-school night, so the two assistant teachers and I carefully planned it together. I really appreciated their advice since they have been through this many times. When Tuesday night arrived I was glad I would finally have the opportunity to meet all the parents and explain the exciting curriculum in our classroom.

I began the evening with introductions, then the three of us taught the parents one of our favorite class movement songs, "Five Little Ducks." I casually pointed out the learning opportunities in this song: vocabulary and syntax development, counting skills, motor coordination, and so on.

Next we presented a slide show of our daily schedule. We made sure that each child was shown in at least one slide. As we showed the slides, we took turns describing our daily activities. I again casually mentioned many of the learning opportunities, especially in early reading and math. I pointed out the developmental progression of early literacy acquisition and what to expect generally at this age. Throughout the presentation I emphasized how much children learn through play, trying to give a good overview of developmentally appropriate practice.

From their smiles and comments, I could tell the parents loved the slide show. They were thrilled to see what their child was doing during the day, and they enjoyed seeing their child's picture, of course!

For the next part of the evening, we had set up some art and science materials that the children are particularly interested in. I explained the educational value in each activity. I had also made cards, which I left next to each set of materials, that highlighted the learning objectives. The parents explored a few of these materials, and then we gathered as a group one more time to end the evening. I asked the parents if they had any questions.

Daniel's father spoke up first: "What are you doing to get the children ready for school? Will they be ready for kindergarten with all this playtime?"

I smiled, trying to keep the tension out of my voice, and explained once again the academic value of the materials and activities the 3-year-olds work on.

Tariq's mother raised her hand next. "But how about learning to write their letters and numbers? Couldn't they spend some time practicing these? Tariq loves the workbooks we have at home," she said.

Daniel's mother quickly joined the discussion: "I can look into getting some computer software for the class. We have *Jump Start Kindergarten* at home that Daniel works on."

This time I took a deep breath—I was starting to get nervous. Hadn't these parents heard anything I had said? The children are 3-year-olds. They still have two more years before they even get to kindergarten! I couldn't believe the parents really wanted to push their children into academics so early!

I tried hard to smile as Beth's mother entered the discussion before I could answer.

"I think it's important to teach children that school is hard work and should be taken seriously. Learning is not all fun and they need to get used to it. I'm worried about all this playtime."

I began to panic. I thought we had planned everything so well and I had explained the value in developmentally appropriate practice. Clearly I had not gotten through to some of the parents.

I lost my confidence and confusion set in. Was I wrong? I was having a hard time putting myself in the parents' position. I knew I had to intervene in this discussion quickly, before it got out of hand. I looked out at the parents' faces looming before me. What else could I say?

Discussion questions

1. What advice can you give Gail? What else can she say to the parents to explain developmentally appropriate practice? What else could she have planned for the evening to help them understand?

2. Retell this case from the perspective of a parent. Does this help you come up with other ideas about what to say to parents? Why do you think they are so concerned about academics?

3. What role, if any, should the director of the center play in explaining the curriculum to parents? What could the director do to help Gail?

4. What is developmentally appropriate for 3-year-olds? What can you expect in terms of social, emotional, intellectual, and physical development? David Elkind has proposed that we are pushing children with our inappropriate expectations. Do you agree?

5. What role do cultural expectations play in parents' understanding of developmentally appropriate practice? How is developmentally appropriate practice influenced by the cultural context of the school and the children? Could Gail be wrong?

"These Parents Just Don't Care!"

Lenore is extremely frustrated by the parents of her first-graders. They don't help with homework, come to the open house, or provide adequate care for their children. How can she build a positive relationship with parents when it seems like they just don't care?

I hung up the phone one more time, trying to track down DeAngelo's mother or anybody in his family. I'd now gone through six phone numbers trying to find someone who could take a message or knows how to get in touch with the family. How am I supposed to keep up positive communication with the families of my students when they don't seem to care!

DeAngelo is really struggling through our work in first grade this year. He is easily distracted, can't sit in his chair even for a few minutes, and has a lot of trouble paying attention. He doesn't seem to recognize any letters or letter sounds, and his speech development seems slow.

I desperately want to talk to someone from his family so I can refer DeAngelo to our child study team for more testing. I have sent home many notes asking his mother to call me or stop by the school at any time for a conference. I have gotten no answers, which doesn't surprise me since DeAngelo never brings in any completed homework assignments.

We had our open house last week. Of the 27 families in my class, only eight parents showed up to learn more about what their children will do in school this year. I should know by now not to expect more, but I keep hoping. I've spent 14 years at this school, and I've seen the neighborhood change dramatically. What used to be a pleasant, working-class Italian and Polish neighborhood has been slowly changing into what I'd have to call a slum. There are boarded-up buildings, drug dealers on the corners, high-school-age kids hanging out at the little markets on the corners. I can tell you that I'm glad our school has a fenced parking lot or I'd be afraid to go out to my car.

I always wanted to teach in an urban school. Because I grew up in the city, I had no illusions about how hard it would be. I kept my positive outlook longer than most of my colleagues at the school, but somehow this year I seem to have more than my fair share of parents who just don't care.

Rachel, for example, comes to school with a can of soda and a candy bar almost every day. I've sent notes home about good nutrition, and we've done class activities that focus on healthy eating. How can a parent of a 6-year-old give her soda and candy for lunch?

Joe and his four siblings live with their grandmother because their mother is a heroin addict. Mary lives with her 70-year-old grandmother because her mother is in prison for murder. Elsie lives with her grandmother and six siblings because her parents abandoned them.

DeAngelo is not the only child who doesn't do any homework. Many of the kids don't know the alphabet or their numbers. How can I possibly teach them all they need to know when their families don't help at home? It's no wonder these kids are not better prepared for school. I don't know how they are going to make it to second grade.

I've heard people argue on the local radio call-in show that the government should require a license to be a parent. Well I for one think that may be a good

idea. I see too much neglect and so many bad choices that parents make. These kids deserve better than they are getting!

Discussion questions

1. Do you agree with Lenore that the government should have a license for parents? Why or why not?

2. What do you think Lenore can do to help a child like DeAngelo when she can't contact the family? What social services or other support systems are available in your school or community? Does the teacher have an ethical obligation in this case to report neglect or suspected child abuse?

3. Can you give Lenore any advice about teaching a class that has little family support? How can she adapt her instructional practices to better meet the children's needs?

4. What role do teacher expectations play in this case? Do you think Lenore's fear that many of the children won't make it to second grade can become a self-fulfilling prophecy?

5. What strategies can Lenore and her school use to reach out to families and help them become partners in their children's education? In what ways do schools discourage parent involvement?

Getting Rid of the Pacifier

Susan feels that 3½-year-old Stephanie should get rid of her pacifier completely. Stephanie doesn't seem to need it while she is at school, and Susan would like to talk to her parents about taking it away.

"Good morning, Stephanie," I say with a big smile on my face. Stephanie smiles back behind the rim of the pacifier in her mouth. I also greet her babysitter Jenna and ask how everything is.

"Oh, we're doing great today. Come and give me a hug goodbye, Stephanie!"

The two of them hug and Jenna dashes out the door.

Jenna cares for Stephanie four days a week because Stephanie's parents work long hours. The two seem to have a very positive relationship. I worry, however, about the time when Jenna might want to leave for another job.

As Stephanie takes off her coat, I approach her. "Hey Stephanie, let's put your pacifier back in your cubby, okay?" She readily agrees, sticking it into the plastic bag on her shelf. Then she trots off to the block corner to build with her friend Kelly. Most days Stephanie goes all day without seeming to remember her pacifier. Only occasionally, when she is tired or frustrated, does she ask for it. But as soon as it's time to go home, she rushes over to her cubby and pulls it out of the bag.

Whether Jenna or one of her parents drops her off, every morning when Stephanie arrives, the pacifier is stuck in her mouth. I really think that at age 3½ Stephanie is way too old to walk around with a pacifier. I also worry that it may be ruining her teeth. She's starting to get a gap between the two top front teeth and I think it's from using the pacifier so much. There are two or three other children in the center who have pacifiers, but they are much younger than Stephanie. None of the children in our room has one anymore, although a few of the kids do suck their thumbs at naptime.

I feel that Stephanie is ready to give up the pacifier entirely. I want to talk to her parents about taking it away, but I don't know what to say. I don't see them very often because Jenna usually drops off and picks up. Therefore, I haven't gotten to know the parents very well.

I worry also that it can't be good emotionally for Stephanie to spend so much time with the babysitter. I think that, because Stephanie's parents can't be with her as much as they'd like, they give in to anything she wants, including the pacifier, because they feel guilty and don't want to make her unhappy.

I wish I knew what my role should be. Should I talk to the parents about taking the pacifier away? Am I overstepping my bounds as a teacher? I really do think Stephanie would be better off without it. I have her best interest in mind!

Discussion questions

1. Do you agree with Susan that Stephanie is too old to use a pacifier? What do you know about child development that supports your answer?

2. If a parent or caregiver decides that a pacifier or another comfort item should be taken away, what do you think is the most appropriate way to do so? Some people feel that comfort items should never be taken away. How do you think they rationalize this viewpoint?

3. What role do you consider appropriate for Susan to take in this case? Do you think she should discuss her concerns with the parents or stay out of parenting issues?

4. Do you think that spending too much time with a babysitter can be detrimental to a child? If yes, how would you define too much time?

5. How can the views of Loris Malaguzzi, the founder of the Reggio Emilia approach to early education, give us a different perspective on the roles of children, teachers, and families in this case?

Homework Hassles

Hannah feels that her homework assignments do not meet the diverse needs of all the children in her second-grade class. She wonders how she can satisfy the district mandate for homework assignments and still attend to the children's individual needs.

During my teacher preparation courses at college, I made up my mind that I would not give homework. I felt that six-and-a-half hours of school work each day was enough. By the time most kids get home, they are tired and so are their parents. There is enough stress in everyday life without the added pressure of homework. Besides, I had read some articles stating there is no relationship between homework and achievement in elementary school. In other words, homework doesn't really help kids do better in school.

Another thing that really bothers me is that it seems so unfair to the kids whose parents can't or won't help with homework. When I was a child, my father was an alcoholic and my mother did the best she could with the stress that his drinking caused the family. I was on my own trying to do my homework, and I usually helped my little sister with hers too. So I empathize with the kids who come to school with no homework.

During my first few years of teaching, I worked at a child care center where the only homework the children ever had was remembering to bring in an object to share that started with the letter of the week. If a child forgot, we had a supply of items he could choose from, so no one was left out.

This year I finally got a public school position, which I wanted primarily because of the increase in salary and benefits. I miss the preschoolers with whom I worked, but I am excited about the new challenges of my second-grade class.

The school is in a large suburban township that prides itself on academic achievement. I think it has the highest SAT scores in the county, or something like that. I started out the year basically giving no homework, but by the end of the second week, a few other teachers made it clear to me that there was a district and school policy about homework. In second grade I was expected to assign and grade 20 minutes of work each night. To my horror, some of the teachers even gave assignments on Fridays.

Well, I felt that I was compromising my beliefs, but I had to follow the district guidelines. I surveyed the homework the other second-grade teachers were giving—mostly worksheets from our language arts and math series. I followed suit partly because I was exhausted just trying to keep up with the day-to-day planning I had to do. Everything was new to me in second grade, and in many ways I felt like a brand new teacher again.

Although I wasn't happy about the homework situation, other things were more pressing so I basically didn't worry about it. During my first afternoon of parent conferences in November, however, the problem gained importance. First, Jason's mom said that she thought the homework was not challenging enough for her son, and she was worried about him doing well on his year-end tests to qualify for the gifted and talented program. I knew that Jason was indeed very bright, but I didn't see the point in putting so much academic pressure on him.

Next, Evelyn's parents said they were concerned because it often took Evelyn an hour or more to do her homework each night.

Giving It Some Thought

They said it was a real battle to get her to do it at all. She complained and procrastinated and they ended up threatening or punishing her. I was distressed at the thought of Evelyn getting so upset over a couple of worksheets.

I decided to get more information so I could ask each parent at the parent-teacher conferences how his or her child was doing with the homework. What I found out really surprised me. Of the 18 parents I talked to, five thought the homework was not challenging enough and wanted their children to do more. (I didn't think any parent would want *more* homework for their child!) Four parents said the homework was a real struggle for their children. What was especially surprising was that some of these four were the parents of my higher achieving children. The other nine parents were neutral. They either said it was okay or seemed unsure. The children of a few of these parents often missed homework assignments. The parents of many of the other kids who regularly don't bring in homework didn't come for conferences. Not surprising, I guess.

So now I'm very confused about what to do. The other second-grade teachers seem so secure in what they give as homework assignments. In fact they say it's the only way they can cover all the workbook pages they need to before the standardized testing. But I think there must be a better solution.

How can I follow the district guidelines for homework in second grade and still meet the individual needs of my children and their parents?

Discussion questions

1. What do you think is the value of homework? Do you agree with Hannah that it should not be assigned at all in second grade? Why or why not?

2. What do you think Hannah should do about her homework assignments? Can you think of any solutions that would help her follow the individual needs of the children and still meet the district mandate for homework?

3. What do you remember about homework from your own schooling? Is the feeling positive, negative, or neutral? Why? How do you think your experiences with homework have shaped your views as a teacher?

4. Lev Vygotsky sees learning as stemming from the social environment. How can his views of learning help us make decisions about homework?

5. Check with various teachers or school districts in your area. What are their policies on homework? How do they differ? Do any of the policies provide information that could help Hannah in this case?

Resources for further reading

Edwards, C., L. Gandini, & G. Forman, eds. 1993. *The hundred languages of children: The Reggio Emilia approach to early childhood education.* Norwood, NJ: Ablex.

Gandini, L. 1993. Fundamentals of the Reggio Emilia approach to early childhood education. *Young Children* 49 (1): 4–8.

Malaguzzi, L. 1993. For an education based on relationships. *Young Children* 49 (1): 9–12.

> These three resources provide valuable and thorough information about the Reggio Emilia approach to early childhood education. They offer an overview of the general principles of Reggio Emilia for readers who are not familiar with the approach, while also painting a picture of what life in Reggio Emilia programs is like for teachers, children, and families.

Eggen, P., & D. Kauchak. 1998. *Educational psychology: Windows on classrooms.* 4th ed. Upper Saddle River, NJ: Merrill.

> Like almost any educational psychology textbook, this book has a chapter on the development of cognition and language that provides a basic look at Jean Piaget's and Lev Vygotsky's theories. Another chapter covering personal, social, and emotional development gives a succinct explanation of Erik Erikson's and Lawrence Kohlberg's theoretical frameworks.

Elkind, D. 1981. *The hurried child.* Reading, MA: Addison-Wesley.

Elkind, D. 1987. *Miseducation: Preschoolers at risk.* New York: Knopf.

> In these two volumes David Elkind, a prominent child advocate, argues that society is hurrying preschoolers and miseducating them by providing inappropriate experiences and holding inappropriate expectations for young children.

Erikson, E.H. 1963. *Childhood and society.* New York: Norton.

> This landmark work on the social significance of childhood has greatly influenced modern understanding of human development. Outlining eight stages in emotional development, this book also explains a psychoanalytic perspective of early childhood. Included are case studies and anecdotes to illustrate the main ideas.

Faber, A., & E. Mazlish. 1995. *How to talk so kids can learn at home and in school.* New York: Rawson.

> This very readable book, illustrated with cartoon vignettes, focuses on strategies for positive communication and problem solving with children that also work well with adults. It includes a valuable chapter on the parent-teacher relationship.

Kohlberg, L. 1984. *Essays on moral development, volume 2: The psychology of moral development.* New York: Harper & Row.

Kohlberg, L. 1969. Stage and sequence: The cognitive-developmental approach to socialization. In *Handbook of socialization theory and research,* ed. D.A. Goslin, 347–480. Chicago: Rand McNally.

> These early texts give the background on Kohlberg's theory of moral development. They describe Kohlberg's clinical use of moral dilemmas to assess level of thinking and stage of moral reasoning. The ideas put forth in

these works are derived from Jean Piaget's views of moral development and have been reexamined and redefined by many researches and theorists since their publication.

Piaget, J. & B. Inhelder. 1969. *The psychology of the child.* London: Rouledge & Kegan Paul.
    This volume translates and synthesizes Piaget's original writings about how the concrete and symbolic cognitive processes develop from infancy through adolescence.

Powell, D.R. 1989. *Families and early childhood programs.* Washington, DC: NAEYC.
    This in-depth review of the literature includes an overview of the rationale for working with parents and links research on home-school relationships with practical strategies.

Reguero de Atiles, J.T., D.A. Stegelin, & J.K. Long. 1997. Biting behavior among preschoolers: A review of the literature and survey of practitioners. *Early Childhood Education Journal* 25 (2): 101–05.
    This article reviews research on the incidence of biting behaviors, reactions to biting, and strategies to cope with biting. The authors also report on a survey of child care providers' views on whether biting is a normal developmental behavior and how caregivers' philosophies relate to their handling of biting incidents in their programs.

Slaby, R.G., W.C. Roedell, D. Arezzo, & K. Hendrix. 1995. *Early violence prevention: Tools for teachers of young children.* Washington, DC: NAEYC.
    The authors describe practical ways to handle children's aggression and help children become assertive, nonviolent problem solvers.

Stone, J.G. 1989. *Teacher-parent relationships.* Washington, DC: NAEYC.
    This small booklet provides practical guidance and beautiful photographs on developing warm, respectful relationships with preschool parents.

Vygotsky, L. 1978. *Mind in society: The development of higher psychological processes.* Cambridge, MA: Harvard University Press.
    This classic work provides a scholarly foundation for Vygotsky's psychology of learning, including the ideas of the zone of proximal development, language as a social process, the role of egocentric speech, and the relationship between intrapsychological and interpsychological development.

2

Challenges of Curriculum

How Can I Get My
Director to Understand?

Sheila, a teacher of infants and toddlers, is frustrated in trying to implement developmentally appropriate practice when her director demands that she provide what Sheila considers to be inappropriate art activities.

We have 12 developmentally delayed children; a staff-child ratio of one to four; a well-lit, spacious, organized classroom; toys in abundance; and adequate supplies to suit every need. Doesn't this sound like the ideal classroom? Well, what is missing from the description is the method of teaching expected by our director, Diane, who holds a degree in psychology but has no background in early childhood education. She has no idea what is developmentally appropriate for children from birth through age 3.

When I assumed this teaching position I was so excited, bursting with new ideas to implement in my classroom. I had many opportunities and took advantage of them by doing all sorts of fun, creative, cognitively stimulating activities with my children. I was careful that the children were challenged at the appropriate developmental levels and that they felt successful at whatever they did.

But this didn't last long. One ominous day my lesson plan was rejected by Diane. For the art activity, I had planned "toddler graffiti," allowing the children to scribble on different surfaces using various media. Diane said, "This is not art. The parents expect *real* art to come home; they don't want to see scribbling. They need to recognize what the picture is."

"But the children need opportunities to explore and experiment with different art materials. It's not developmentally appropriate to expect them to do representational art," I pleaded.

"Well, cut out some patterns and have the children color them instead," Diane curtly replied.

Deciding I wasn't getting anywhere with my argument, I backed down. Although I did cut out patterns, I let the children have some freedom and creativity in how they colored them. This activity was nothing like the one I had originally envisioned, and I felt frustrated.

The following week I tried once again. This time I planned to have the children explore fingerpainting using different textures. I had coffee grounds, cornmeal, sand, and flour for them to add to the paint. I fully expected another argument with Diane about representational art. Instead she focused on the mess.

Diane came into my classroom just as one group of children was going to the sink to wash up and another group was coming to the activity center to get started. "Sheila, you can't make this kind of mess in here. There is paint everywhere and I'm afraid the kids are going to get it all over their clothes. The smocks can't protect them from this much paint. Aren't there some art activities you can do that don't make such a mess?"

I mumbled something about cleaning up when I was done, but I could tell Diane was not satisfied with my answer. I decided to find out what the other teachers were doing.

I was surprised that I hadn't noticed before the kind of art hanging on their walls and in the hall. It was typical cut-and-paste artwork that all looked the same. I spoke to some teachers about Diane wanting art projects that were copied from the teacher's model, and they did not seem to have a problem with this. Perhaps they think this type of patterned art is an easy way out. To me it seems that they are using the same art activities year after year and failing to use their imaginations to implement new ideas.

Giving It Some Thought

At this point I don't know what to do. I'm torn between my enthusiasm for teaching and the frustration of not being able to teach the way I think is appropriate. I struggle through days when Diane makes routine checks to see that I am following our daily schedule and lesson plans without deviation. I am losing the opportunity to make use of teachable moments.

How can I get Diane to understand what developmentally appropriate practice really means, especially in promoting creativity?

Discussion questions

1. What *does* developmentally appropriate practice really mean? How would you explain it to someone who doesn't seem to understand? Does everyone agree? What other viewpoints on developmentally appropriate practice can you find besides the NAEYC position statement? For example, what are the art experiences like in the Reggio Emilia approach?

2. What education and experience should the director of a child care center have? What are the regulations in your state? Do you think they are adequate? What are the national accreditation standards for directors?

3. Should teachers always be able to teach the way they want to? What role should the director play in deciding curriculum activities?

4. What is developmentally appropriate art for toddlers? Why do you think Sheila feels that patterned art is inappropriate? What do you think are the parents' perspectives in this case?

5. What advice could you give Sheila? Brainstorm as many possible options as you can think of to deal with this problem.

Curriculum Overload

Mariko is having difficulty planning curriculum activities for her class of 3-year-olds. With all the activities that are required of teachers in the child care center, Mariko doesn't know when she can do the activities related to her weekly themes. She wonders if there is just too much to fit in.

I'm sitting here on my bed on Sunday night trying to plan for the upcoming week.

I have a wonderful class of 3-year-olds, 15 children who keep me on my toes. They are filled with curiosity and wonder, always eager and ready to try new things. They seem to have an insatiable appetite for exploration and discovery. So it may seem that planning curriculum activities for them should be easy. My problem is not finding activities that the children would like to do, but rather finding the time in my daily schedule for all the activities I have to do with the children and the ones I want to add.

Our child care center has a reputation for preparing children academically. The emphasis is on getting children ready for later schooling. Our director has put together a schoolwide curriculum framework planned six months in advance that all the teachers use.

Each week we cover one letter of the alphabet and one number. There is a learning center activity based on these each day, such as number bingo and alphabet lotto. Every month we cover one shape and one nursery rhyme. Each day of the week there is also a class taught by a specialist. Monday is science, Tuesday is gym, Wednesday is cooking, Thursday is computers, and Friday is music.

Teachers are given a specific theme around which to organize and integrate their activities each week. It was especially tough to find the right activities for our last few themes: snowmen, popcorn, and polar bears. In addition, many parents have been requesting homework. I'm trying also to plan appropriate activities for the children to do at home.

By the time I put the letter, number, shape, nursery rhyme, and specials into my plans, I feel as if there is no time left to do some of the more open-ended choice activities I'd like to provide for my children.

It's a bit unclear to me why all the age groups in the center must focus on the same themes, letters, numbers, and so on. Shouldn't there be different focuses for different age groups? Even the 2-year-olds follow this same curriculum.

I'm not sure that I really know what's best, however. I have just gone back to school to continue my education and eventually get my bachelor's degree and state teacher certification. Previously I earned some credits at the county community college, and I have my Child Development Associate credential, which I earned at classes offered by our county resource-and-referral agency.

I just love my courses—it's so meaningful to learn something in class and then apply it to my real work. Unfortunately it also frustrates me a bit. When I learn about the types of activities and scheduling that are considered developmentally appropriate, I begin to wonder about all the activities I am required to add to my program.

I really believe that we need to work hard preparing children for kindergarten, getting the academic skills that the children will need later under their belts. But maybe there's a better way to do it than focusing on required activities and themes.

Discussion questions

1. What do you consider the advantages of having all the teachers in a child care center follow the same curriculum framework? The disadvantages?

2. What are the advantages and disadvantages of using curriculum themes? Are some themes more appropriate than others? If so, what makes a good theme for curriculum development? Besides themes, what other ways are there to develop curriculum? For example, how does this program compare to a Montessori program for 3-year-olds?

3. What advice would you give Mariko? Brainstorm all the possible choices that she has and try to envision the outcome of each.

4. How important is it for child care centers and preschool programs to get children ready for kindergarten? What does it mean to be ready for kindergarten?

5. Mariko is having difficulty fitting in all the activities she is required to do. What do you think is an appropriate daily schedule for 3-year-olds? Try to plan a few different schedules or ask teachers what schedules they use. Evaluate the effectiveness of each. Can you identify general guidelines for an effective daily schedule?

Teaching a Second Language

Jackie debates with her colleagues the appropriateness of meeting the state curriculum standards for second-language learning in their preschool programs. She begins to incorporate Spanish into her program, only to have a parent suggest they include French also. She wonders what is an appropriate second-language curriculum for preschool.

Our state recently adopted core curriculum standards that call for instruction in world languages throughout elementary school. Most public schools in our area have begun putting in place programs to teach a second language beginning in kindergarten. These programs are given as specials in which a language teacher works with the children for one period once a week.

At our local early childhood professional association board meetings over the past few months, we have informally discussed how much responsibility child care centers and preschool programs should take for addressing these core curriculum standards. Donna, one of my colleagues, got a lot of agreement when she said, "We have worked so hard to fight for play-based child-centered programs, I worry now that we will be forced to introduce skills instruction that is not developmentally appropriate."

"But what is developmentally appropriate when it comes to second-language learning? Does anyone know the best way for preschoolers to learn a second language?" responded Annette.

"I think the only way it can be done is to integrate it into everything the kids do. I just feel that isolated instruction won't work. They'll learn a few words but never be able to really say anything," Maria added.

Donna replied, "But that would mean having teachers who are bilingual. I know we have a few bilingual teachers in our programs, but they wouldn't be enough."

Janet gave us a different view: "I really think we should just leave it alone. We have enough to do getting the kids ready socially and emotionally and introducing basic concepts for reading and math. I just think preschoolers don't need second-language instruction. They can wait until they get to kindergarten in the public schools. It's not going to hurt them to wait."

This brought another round of discussion, and it seemed we didn't reach much of a consensus except to acknowledge that we needed to know more about the best way to introduce a second language to young children. We were all concerned about a second language being taught in a skills-based pull-out program for which a specialist would come to the school, but we didn't know a better alternative.

The week following that discussion, a parent in my program for 3- and 4-year-olds mentioned to me that she speaks Spanish. She wondered if she could help me introduce Spanish to the children. I was struck by how important our professional discussion was— clearly the parents in our area were aware of the new second-language programs in the public schools. I told Mrs. Hernandez that I'd love to have her help and that I'd get back to her with a plan.

I went home to consider the circumstances. The bilingual parent's offer presented a challenge and an opportunity that I couldn't pass up. I finally decided that I would start off with a plan that was small in scope but that fit my philosophy. We began to incorporate Spanish into our music activities. Together Mrs. Hernandez and I came up with some appropriate songs and chants to include in our program.

After two weeks I felt confident that this was a positive addition to our program. The children were enjoying the songs and learning new words quickly. I began to think about how I could extend this and include Spanish in other areas of our program. Then yesterday Mrs. Miller, another parent, approached me after class. "I noticed the children are learning some words in Spanish. Kyle is enjoying that. I wanted to let you know that I speak French and I'd love to help you teach the children French."

I was taken by surprise and didn't know how to answer. Another language? Wouldn't that be too much? How could I integrate both French and Spanish? Wouldn't it confuse the children?

On the other hand, what can I tell Mrs. Miller? I don't want to hurt her feelings or give the impression that Spanish is preferred over French or any other language.

I feel as if I've gotten myself into a mess. I can't wait until our next board meeting to ask my colleagues for advice!

Discussion questions

1. What is developmentally appropriate second-language instruction for young children? Try to determine how to find out this information and what advice you would give at the next board meeting.

2. What factors should be considered in deciding which second language to introduce to young children?

3. What options do you think Jackie has for responding to Mrs. Miller's request? What is the best choice?

4. Jackie mentions attending board meetings at her local early childhood organization. What professional organizations for early childhood educators are available in your area? Nationally? Statewide?

5. Has your state developed core curriculum standards? If so, in what ways can preschool programs support the standards that have been identified for elementary school? Should early childhood educators be concerned about supporting these standards? Why or why not? Compare the philosophy of John Dewey with the concept of establishing core curriculum standards. How are they different?

Developmentally Appropriate Practice in the Primary Grades?

Carrie wonders how she can implement developmentally appropriate practice in her first grade when she has a large class, not enough materials, and administrative pressure to prepare the children for standardized testing.

I was an accountant for about five years before I decided that I was really not happy with my job. In the back of my mind I had always harbored the goal of becoming a teacher, but when I was in college, teaching just didn't seem a wise career path—the pay wasn't great and the status was low. When I got older (and perhaps wiser), I realized that I wanted to at least give teaching a chance.

I earned a master's degree in early childhood education that lead to my state teaching certification. When I graduated, however, I had difficulty finding a teaching job, especially since I already had kids of my own and couldn't easily relocate or commute long distances.

I finally found a job in a large urban district close by. I was offered a first-grade position, and I jumped at the chance. I love young children and I felt well prepared for a first-grade classroom.

I spent the summer rereading many of my college textbooks, preparing materials, and gathering teacher's idea books. I couldn't wait to get into the actual classroom (in this district the teachers are not allowed in the school building until the day before the children start).

When I reported the first day, I think I had the same feelings the kids have when starting school again: excitement mixed with anxiety and anticipation. I opened the door to my classroom and stood looking for a long time at the quiet, mostly empty space. The room had large windows, high ceilings, and hardwood floors scratched from many years of heavy use. The old, old radiator spewed out heat in waves from under the windows. The stained blinds were pulled down so I could see the bent and broken slats. I immediately began planning what I would do with the space to brighten it up and make it seem more like home.

I spent the better part of the day arranging the 29 desks (yes, I was shocked to find 29 children on my class list!). I put them in groups of fours so I could also fit in learning centers. I soon ran into some problems.

I wanted the library corner to be the highlight of the room; however, there were no bookshelves anywhere. I had begun my own collection of books that I hoped to add to from the library, but what would I do about bookshelves? I also had no shelves for my collection of math manipulatives.

There was only one round table in addition to my huge desk and the children's desks. By the end of the day, I had center materials set up to use on the kids' desks; it would work, but it sure wasn't the perfect classroom I had seen in videos in my college classes.

With the first few months of school coming to an end, I've found a few more obstacles in my path toward developmentally appropriate practice in first grade. I now have 31 children—we've squeezed in a few more desks. I never imagined how hard it would be to have that many children in a class. Just getting enough supplies for them is a problem, not to mention teaching them how to work in groups or use centers independently.

I've also discovered that not all the other first-grade teachers in the building agree with my approach. They have been very helpful and friendly, but most seem to think centers are impossible to use in first grade. Much of their instruction is whole-group teacher-directed lessons. They also emphasize the need to use the textbooks adopted by the district and to get the kids ready for taking the standardized tests in the spring.

Luckily I've found a friend and colleague in Linda, a kindergarten teacher whose class is right down the hall. We've shared suggestions for centers, reading activities, art projects, and most of all for keeping up with the tons of paperwork required by the administration. Linda has also helped me become familiar with the policies and politics of the school. I don't know what I would have done without her.

Linda seems better able to use developmentally appropriate practices in her classroom, perhaps because she teaches kindergarten. There is a strong perception that first grade should be "real school," with kids sitting quietly at desks writing carefully in their workbooks. Nor does Linda in kindergarten have standardized testing hanging over her head. Unfortunately, because in this district standardized testing begins in first grade, I feel great pressure to run my classroom the way the other first-grade teachers do.

Last week my supervisor came to observe my class. The children were working at centers at the time. I had one small group doing guided reading with me, one group working on a science experiment, another group working on simple addition problems with counters, and the rest of the kids either working on the assigned pages in their workbooks or making an art project connected to our fall theme.

The children were quite noisy. I'm still working hard on getting them to use "inside" voices. They also needed a lot of my attention. I had to keep interrupting my guided reading lesson to answer questions or redirect some of the children. My supervisor was kind and smiled a lot, but her words still stung: "It seems like you need to get more control over the children and make sure they are quieter and on task."

In some ways I agree with my supervisor. But I know also that children in first grade learn best with developmentally appropriate practices. I just don't know if it's possible to use such practices in this school where I have 31 children in my class, not enough furniture or supplies, and pressure from my peers and supervisor to prepare the children for standardized testing.

Discussion questions

1. What does Carrie mean by "developmentally appropriate practices in first grade"? What would that encompass? There are people in early childhood education who feel that we should reconceptualize developmentally appropriate practice by looking at children through a lens other than that of developmental psychology. How, for example, might you look at this case from the view of feminist theory?

2. Do you agree with Carrie that first-graders need developmentally appropriate practice as much as kindergartners? What difference, if any, should there be between kindergarten and first grade?

3. Given the obstacles that Carrie describes, such as large class size and limited materials, do you think it is possible for her to be developmentally appropriate? What advice could you give her?

4. Do you think it is appropriate to use standardized testing in first grade? Should Carrie "prepare" the children for these tests?

5. What do you think Carrie should plan to do when her supervisor comes for the next visit?

To Test or Not to Test?

Miss Pulaski questions whether it is appropriate to use standardized testing in kindergarten. She has helped form a group of teachers and parents who want to change the district's policy about testing. They wonder where to begin in developing a plan to present to the school board.

"What is this, Miss Pulaski?" Katie asks innocently, pointing at one of the pictures in her test booklet.

"Just do the best you can, Katie. I can't help you," I answer with frustration. It is so hard not being able to help the children, particularly when they don't really understand the questions. But this is a standardized test with explicit instructions about what I am allowed to say and not say. To me it seems almost akin to child abuse.

As I look around the room, I see Bruce and Christopher wiggling in their seats so much that I'm afraid they're disturbing the kids next to them. Jackie has been biting her nails since the testing began, and Kristel has spent the whole time twirling her hair around her finger. Amad is chewing on the collar of his shirt, and already three children have asked to go to the bathroom. Every year I get more concerned as I watch the stress this test causes the children.

Our school district has used standardized testing in kindergarten for many years. The test scores are used to place children in classes for first grade and to determine which reading groups they will be in. They are also used to determine who participates in the gifted and talented program and who receives basic skills instruction. But there are a number of teachers in our district who feel that this kind of testing is inappropriate in kindergarten or even in the primary grades.

Because there is so much pressure to have the children perform well on these tests, our entire curriculum has become focused on them. At the beginning of the year, our principal gives us lists of all the concepts covered on our grade level's test. We are expected to incorporate them into the curriculum throughout the year. Of course the standardized test assesses only math and literacy skills, so other subjects such as science, art, music, and social studies get much less emphasis in our curriculum.

We also get test-preparation booklets to use with the children. The booklets expose the children to the format of the test, teach them how to color in the test bubbles, and review some of the tests' general content.

A good portion of our class time each spring is used to teach children how to take the test. In my view this time would be better spent helping children learn new concepts and broadening the curriculum.

A few teachers and I have recently formed a group that is working on a plan to change the district's policies about standardized testing. We want to go before the school board with a written proposal by the end of the school year. Most of us are early childhood teachers, but we have recruited a few parents as well.

It was hard to find parents who agreed with us, however. Most of the parents we approached about this issue felt the standardized tests are important indications of how their kids are doing compared to other children. They also felt that the tests hold teachers accountable for what the children are supposed to learn in each grade.

This information has helped our group realize how much work we need to do to convince parents that standardized tests are not the best assessment method, and we are trying to come up with a strong approach. We want to document what the limitations of standardized testing are and especially show how unreliable such testing is for young children. We also want to show that using test scores to group children for instruction is not appropriate in the early grades.

We realize that we will have to present an alternative to testing. We can't give up assessment altogether, so we need a plan for other kinds of assessment that will be less stressful for the children and will give more accurate information. We are somewhat overwhelmed by the task we've set for ourselves, and we are wondering where we should start!

Discussion questions

1. What are the pros and cons of using standardized testing in early childhood?

2. In what ways does standardized testing affect the curriculum in early childhood? How can you relate Michel Foucault's ideas about power relationships in assessment procedures to developmentally appropriate practice in this case? Who decides what the early childhood curriculum covers when standardized tests are used?

3. What advice would you give this group of teachers and parents about preparing a proposal for assessment alternatives to present to the school board? What should they include? What resources will they need?

4. If you were required to give standardized tests in kindergarten, in what ways, if any, would you prepare the children for the tests?

5. What are some alternatives to standardized testing? How could you convince parents that other forms of assessment are more appropriate than standardized testing?

How Much Choice
Do Children Need?

Noelle is having difficulty deciding how to plan the daily schedule for her kindergarten class. She wants to give the children more choice in planning their own activities, but she also needs to cover the district's prescribed curriculum. Because hers is only a half-day program, Noelle is having a tough time fitting more choice into her schedule.

It's the first week of January and we've just returned from a week's vacation. Not surprisingly, my 26 children seem much calmer and more focused than they were right before the holidays. As I look around my organized, carefully managed room, I have a sense of pride in what my kindergartners have learned since September. I'm especially pleased with how well they've learned the routines and procedures for working in centers this year.

I've been teaching kindergarten for three years now. At first I just couldn't handle learning centers. I didn't know how to organize them or get the children to work independently without chaos resulting. I have gradually allowed the kids more freedom to work on projects and activities in small groups.

I recently attended a stimulating conference sponsored by our local affiliate of NAEYC. One session focused on managing learning centers in the classroom. This really struck a chord because I've been trying so hard to get learning centers to work in my classroom.

We spent some time discussing why we want to use centers and all the benefits they provide for children. A lot of the benefits relate to children having choice in what they do and to which centers they go. This got me thinking about my own classroom, and I realized that I still have some changes to make. In light of this conference session, I am not satisfied with the way I am using centers in my class.

In the lounge during lunch one day, I sat down with one of the other new kindergarten teachers. "Kate," I said, "I've been thinking about how I'm using learning centers with the kids in my class. I think I'm not giving them enough choices, but I don't know how to fit in any more with all the curriculum we have to cover."

"I know what you mean, Noelle," Kate replied. "When I was student teaching, I had visions of what my classroom would be like. I wanted it to be just perfect, with the students taking a lot of responsibility for their learning.

"I just didn't expect to have so much curriculum to cover. How can we fit it into the schedule? Between our reading series activities, the phonics workbooks, the math workbooks and activities, and then hopefully fitting in science, social studies, and art or music once in a while, I feel like there's no time to let the kids play or even choose what to do. What if they don't choose the centers that I'm supposed to cover in the curriculum?

"Especially with our half-day program. I really wish that we had the children for the full day. Sometimes I feel like I'm on a treadmill that's set too fast!" Kate concluded. It was comforting to know that Kate shared some of my frustration.

"Let's look at our schedules and see if we can come up with a better plan," I suggested, quickly jotting down my daily schedule on a piece of scrap paper.

8:45 Collect homework, check work folders, put coats away, etc.

9:00 Group time: calendar, morning message, etc.

9:30 Center time

    1/3 class works with me
    1/3 class works at teacher-planned activity
    1/3 class chooses own activity [this means that kids get choice
       time about every third day]

10:10 Snack

10:30 Read aloud

10:50 Outside activities

11:45 Dismissal

"I've finally gotten the kids comfortable with this schedule, and they manage themselves well. But I don't feel that I'm giving them enough choice time. My schedule seems so teacher-directed."

Kate and I sat together at the table for the next few minutes, looking over the schedule. It was just impossible to figure out what to

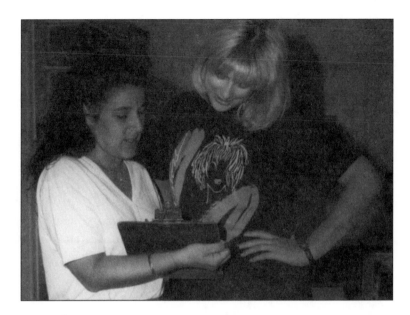

cut out to make more time for choice. How could we do that and still cover all the curriculum materials the district requires?

Discussion questions

1. Looking at Noelle's schedule, what advice can you give her about adding more time for children to make choices and still fitting in the district's curriculum activities?

2. Why is choice important? Is choice more important in kindergarten or in third grade? How about sixth grade or high school? Why?

3. In what ways can you give children choices throughout the day? Brainstorm as many as possible.

4. How many things can you think of that a teacher should consider in planning her daily schedule? How would a half-day schedule differ from a whole day? Give examples.

5. What specifically do you think Noelle has done to get her class well managed and the children using the learning centers productively?

The Reluctant Writer

Gary believes that writing is an important part of the first-grade curriculum. He tries out ideas to stimulate language, encourages invented spelling, and helps the children share with each other. He has one student, John, however, who still doesn't write in his journal. He wonders what more he can do to get John to write.

We have just finished morning activities in our first-grade class, and I have called the students to the rug. Situated in the middle of the U-shaped desk arrangement, this rug is our circle time/group reading area. On the other side of the desks are areas set up as various activity centers. When everyone is settled, I give directions for one student to read, and the rest to join in the reading. I try to model what I want the children to do, so I also join in the reading.

Today's story is about farm animals. The children read the story easily, but I notice that John is very busy with something on the side of the rug. When it is time for the shared reading, he is in the right place and joins in.

John seems to read along quite well with the group. Reading aloud on his own, however, he appears to have stage fright. I don't know if he is shy or if he just lets the group carry him.

After the story is finished, I ask the children which animals would make good pets. They call out the names of the animals we have just read about: horses, cows, ducks, chickens, sheep. As they call them out, I write the names on the chalkboard. I tell the children that we will vote for the best pet and that they can vote more than once. Horses and sheep win.

Next I lead a discussion about why it would be hard to keep these animals as pets in our urban area. I tell the class that I have a pet cat named Cleo that lives in my apartment with me. Before I send them back to their seats for the writing workshop, I tell the children, "Think about what kind of pet you would like to have or what kind of pet you do have. Write down your ideas and we will share them later this afternoon."

After much fumbling through desks, the writing journals are brought out. John is still rummaging through his desk. As I walk around his group, I notice he is playing with his scissors, a pencil, and an eraser.

"John, do you have your journal?" I ask.

He says nothing but pulls his journal out from his desk.

While the students quietly write, I walk around the class looking at their progress, asking them questions, and offering suggestions. Some of the students are off to a good start.

When I come again to John, I notice that he is just staring at the page before him. I hear him ask his neighbor, "What are we supposed to do?"

I'm pleased that Raul answers him and starts a quiet discussion with Larissa and John about pets that they like. I try to encourage the children to share their ideas because I think it helps with their writing.

Raul and Larissa begin writing in between talking to the others, but John just plays with his pencil. I can hear him using descriptive words to describe the pet he'd like to have, but still there is nothing written on his paper. I decide to intervene.

"John, your ideas sound great. Start writing down in your journal just what you told Raul and Larissa."

"Okay," he answers, shifting his body in his seat and grabbing his pencil again.

John is a pleasant child. He is one of the shorter boys in this first-grade class. His movements for the most part are fluid and smooth while at the same time slow and methodical. He is easily distracted and tends to wander at times, but most of the time he pays attention. He relates well socially to the other students and tends to blend into the class.

Once again I make the rounds, stopping to help when asked. A few children ask how to spell a word. Thinking about John's empty paper, I address the whole class. "Don't worry about spelling in your journal. The idea is just to get your thoughts down on paper. Write the word the way it sounds to you. Use your own invented spelling."

"How do we do that?" one of the students asks, so I demonstrate on the board. I ask them what sounds they hear in the word *cat*. Then I write the letters *KT* that they have identified. "You see, if you don't know the spelling, just put down the letters for the sounds you hear."

The students get back to work and I wander over to John's desk. I don't want to make him uncomfortable by focusing on him. John's hands are in his desk playing with his scissors again. I ask him about his pet. When he finishes talking I tell him once more, "Just write that down in your journal now, the best that you can. However you want to spell the words is fine." John just sits there looking at his journal.

Recalling how easily he lets words flow from his mouth, I wonder if there is a fear of seeing his words on paper. Writing is a very personal endeavor. In speech, words are spontaneous and disappear as soon as they are spoken. The written word is carefully chosen, and perhaps John is worried about this.

After walking around to the other groups, I come back to John's desk. The writing workshop period is over and still there is nothing on his paper except a drawing of a cat.

What else can I do for John?

Discussion questions

1. Gary suggests some reasons that might account for John's not writing. What other reasons can you suggest? Brainstorm as many as possible.

2. How well does Gary's classroom reflect the principles identified in the International Reading Association/National Association for the Education of Young Children position statement "Learning to Read and Write: Developmentally Appropriate Practices for Young Children"?

3. Why do you think Gary encourages the children to invent their own spellings? How can he explain this process to parents?

4. Does Gary's literacy instruction in this case demonstrate more of a code-based emphasis to reading instruction or a meaning-based emphasis? What factors did you identify in making this determination?

5. In what way can Vygotsky's ideas about how young children learn to write help us analyze this case?

Resources for further reading

Armington, D. 1997. *The living classroom: Writing, reading, and beyond.* Washington, DC: NAEYC

Through this book we spend time in a first-grade classroom in which children's ideas, writing, and reading thrive. Rather than polarizing whole language and phonics, Armington presents vivid images and examples of an effective classroom.

Bredekamp, S., & C. Copple, eds. 1997. *Developmentally appropriate practice in early childhood programs—Revised edition.* Washington, DC: NAEYC.

This valuable resource spells out the principles underlying developmentally appropriate practice, providing guidelines for classroom decisionmaking and examples of effective and ineffective practices.

Bredekamp, S., & T. Rosegrant, eds. 1992. *Reaching potentials: Appropriate curriculum and assessment for young children—Volume 1.* Washington, DC: NAEYC.

Bredekamp, S., & T. Rosengrant, eds. 1995. *Reaching potentials: Transforming early childhood curriculum and assessment—Volume 2.* Washington, DC: NAEYC.

These two volumes provide a comprehensive overview of national standards and what's important for children to know and be able to do in math, science, health, visual arts, music, social studies, physical education, and language and literacy.

Dewey, J. 1938. *Experience and education.* New York: Touchstone.

One of the more readable of Dewey's statements, this short volume shows how he reformulated his ideas about education as a result of his experience with progressive schools. He addresses the criticism that his theories received after his chief work *Democracy and Education* was published twenty years earlier.

Goldstein, L.S. 1997. *Teaching with love: A feminist approach to early childhood education.* New York: Peter Lang.

In this detailed case study of a primary grade teacher, Goldstein applies feminist thinking to the realities of classroom life. She illustrates through classroom examples what it really means to teach in a manner founded on the ethic of care and shows how caring enters into curricular decisions and teaching practices.

Hendrick, J., ed. 1997. *First steps toward teaching the Reggio way.* Upper Saddle River, NJ: Merrill.

This hands-on guide examines how real teachers in real schools are working to grasp the principles of the Reggio Emilia approach and apply them in their everyday classroom settings. Chapters by leading advocates of the Reggio philosophy are written for practicing and future teachers. Issues explored include the American interpretations of Reggio, examples of working with staff and students to bring about change, and "next steps" in teaching the Reggio way.

International Reading Association (IRA)/NAEYC. 1998. Position Statement. Learning to read and write: Developmentally appropriate practices for young children. *Young Children* 53 (4): 30–46.

This joint position statement of the International Reading Association and NAEYC identifies issues in early literacy instruction, reviews the research literature, and outlines recommended teaching practices. It provides a continuum of the developmental stages in children's early reading and writing.

Jones, E., & J. Nimmo. 1994. *Emergent curriculum.* Washington, DC: NAEYC.

This practical book listens in on the discussions in one center as the teachers and the children move through the year weaving the curriculum as they go. A stimulating, inspiring resource for rethinking curriculum.

Kamii, C., ed. 1990. *Achievement testing in the early grades: Games grown-ups play.* Washington, DC: NAEYC.

This provocative book of essays brings together many voices from the early childhood community calling for a halt to standardized testing in the early grades. While identifying the dilemmas faced in deciding on assessment strategies, the authors outline the negative effects of testing and the possible alternatives.

Kohn, A. 1998. Choices for children: Why and how to let students decide. In *What to look for in a classroom . . . and other essays,* ed. A. Kohn, 249–76. San Francisco: Jossey-Bass.

In his unconventional way Kohn examines the rationale for student choice, what choosing looks like in practice, setting reasonable limits, and barriers to providing choice.

Lubeck, S. 1998. Is developmentally appropriate practice for everyone? *Childhood Education* 74 (5): 283–92.

This article challenges the notion that developmentally appropriate practice represents a common, stable core of knowledge or a consensus of generalizable principles. The author presents alternative views of appropriate practice seen through other cultural and philosophical lenses. The article includes an extensive reference list of readings that provide diverse views of reconceptualizing early childhood education.

Madaus, G., & T. Kellghan. 1996. Curriculum, evaluation, and assessment. In *Handbook of research on curriculum: A project of the American Educational Research Association,* ed. P.W. Jackson, 119–54. New York: Simon & Schuster.

This chapter provides a scholarly overview of Michel Foucault's ideas set in the broader ideological context of evaluation and assessment in schools. In particular the authors discuss Michel Foucault's ideas about the power relationships of institutions and the use of testing as a mechanism of disciplinary power. These ideas are highly relevant to the way social policy in early childhood education is being informed by the use of standardized assessments.

Met, M., & V. Galloway. 1996. Research in foreign language curriculum. In *Handbook of research on curriculum: A project of the American Educational Research Association,* ed. P.W. Jackson, 852–90. New York: Simon & Schuster.

This chapter offers a thorough scholarly overview of why, where, when, by whom, what, and how foreign language curriculum has been and is being used. It makes an excellent starting point for an informed look at how early childhood education might fit into the broad picture of foreign language curriculum.

Montessori, M. 1967. *The discovery of the child.* New York: Ballantine.

Originally published in 1948, this translation of Montessori's writings shares a description and history of her teaching methods, theory of learning, and philosophy. This readable format also provides photos of Montessori materials.

Puckett, M.B., & J.K. Black. 1994. *Authentic assessment of the young child: Celebrating development and learning.* New York: Macmillan.

This comprehensive textbook provides an overview of authentic assessment of young children, including background information on child development, learning, and cultural diversity that is needed to implement authentic assessment. Other chapters include specific authentic assessment strategies.

Schickedanz, J.A. 1998. *Much more than the ABCs: The early stages of reading and writing.* Washington, DC: NAEYC.

Revised and expanded from the popular *More than the ABCs*, this new volume gives a rich picture of children's early steps toward literacy with concrete suggestions for reading aloud with children, setting up a book corner and a writing center, introducing the alphabet in meaningful ways, and appropriate books for young children.

3

Challenges of Classroom Communities

Time-Out

Julissa, a student teacher, questions the cooperating teacher's constant use of the time-out chair to try to control 3-year-old Teresa's behavior. She doesn't think time-out works and wonders what else she can do.

I have found that working with young children is sometimes easier said than done!

I am a student teacher at a private preschool that enrolls about 35 students. The school is in a middle-class community with a wide range of racial, linguistic, and ethnic diversity. In our class we have four African American children, one child from Colombia, three from Puerto Rico, one from Yugoslavia, five Anglo-Americans, and

Teresa, whose family is Portuguese. The cooperating teacher, the classroom aide, and I work well together, but we disagree on issues of discipline and how to deal with defiance.

Like most young children, the children in my class are extremely affectionate. Within the first week I was being hugged more times than I could count. The teacher's aide constantly reminded me that if I was too nice to the children they would take advantage of me. How can you be "too nice" to children? I believe that children need affection and should not feel rejected by their teachers.

I soon found out that Teresa had been giving the teachers a hard time. My cooperating teacher described Teresa's situation for me. She is not quite 4 years old and she started school two months ago. Her mother speaks only Portuguese, and because no one at the school speaks Portuguese, it is hard to communicate with her. Teresa's mother communicated to us that she was having trouble controlling Teresa at home.

Teresa understands Portuguese and some English, but she doesn't speak much of either language, at least to us. Because she is so young, we figured she would begin to pick up English in a matter of time. Well, I've been here eight weeks and the only word I can understand her say is *mommy*. Sometimes at lunch I can make out the word *juice* as she points to it and says "joo." Her mother recently took her to a doctor to have her hearing tested. If I understood the mother correctly, she is to take Teresa back to the doctor in another month.

Besides our concerns about a possible hearing problem, we have also been dealing with Teresa's inappropriate behaviors. She seems to understand all the English she needs to function in the classroom. For example, she knows when to get in line to wash her hands or go to the bathroom, and she responds when we ask her to sit or stand or come here. At any given moment, however, Teresa may stand up, let out a sound, then run around in a circle or up and down the classroom and a moment later sit down again. She has become aggressive as well, throwing things and saying *"No!"* vehemently. If I ask her to do something, she says no and shakes her head and laughs. However, as soon as I walk away, she does what I asked.

The other teachers constantly put Teresa in the time-out chair to sit and "think about" what she did. My problem with this method of discipline is that it doesn't mean anything to her. Teresa seems unfazed by it, and it certainly isn't changing her behavior. I think also the other children are getting the idea that Teresa is a bad kid. I just don't see how putting her in time-out is going to get her to learn the behavior she should be using.

It seems as if the other teachers want to break Teresa's spirit or punish the defiance out of her. I think that caring rather than punishment is what she needs. I think she just enjoys saying the word *no* and feeling the power it gives her.

I began to feel comfortable and secure. The kids seemed willing to share their room with me, and my cooperating teacher got me involved immediately. What a great morning—it was over before I knew it!

At 12:40 children attending the afternoon session came running into the room, laughing a little louder, skipping a little faster, hugging a little tighter. They were a bit more skeptical and cautious about my presence. I helped with snacktime, traveling from table to table, talking with each group, trying to learn a little bit about the children.

After everyone finished snack, there was a run on the bathroom. Bathroom rules had already been firmly established, and everyone must wait his or her turn. Although the kids were really cooperative about this, their bladders weren't. You guessed it, my first accident. Bonnie was very upset and embarrassed by her wet clothes.

"No problem," said Mrs. Harrison. "The nurse keeps extra clothes in her office. I'll take Bonnie down there and clean her up. You can read the kids the same story that we read this morning."

"Great," I thought. "I've got them all to myself."

"Come over to the rug, boys and girls. I've got a story to read to you." I began reading the story, a charming take-off on the traditional *Three Little Pigs*, but with a Southwestern influence.

As I introduced the story, the children began to notice that Mrs. Harrison was not in the room. "Where is she?" I heard whispered several times. But I just kept reading.

The children were becoming restless, and still no Mrs. Harrison.

"'They had hair from their pink little ears right down to the end of their curly little tails,'" I continued to read.

"How about their butts?" I heard from someone sitting in the front row.

I looked up. Expressionless faces stared back. I didn't know who had said it, but the other children seemed not to have heard. Okay, just ignore it, back to the story, I said to myself.

"' . . . They had hair from their pink little ears right down to the end of their curly little tails.'"

"Ms. King, Ms. King!" said a familiar though unidentifiable voice.

I realized Timmy was waving his arm frantically through the air. Should I interrupt the rhythm of the story to acknowledge Timmy? What if he has to go to the bathroom? I wondered. I didn't think I could handle another accident. I decided to answer him.

"What, Timmy?"

As soon as I saw the look on his face, I knew that I had made my first major mistake. I realized where I had heard that voice before— the "butt" comment.

"What about his weenie? Was that hairy too? Did the pigs have hairy weenies, Ms. King? Did they, huh? Did they have hairy weenies, oooh, Ms. King?"

Oh, no. He was asking me about the pigs' private parts! What was I supposed to do?

My first day of teaching and I'd already had a wet pants situation and a "privates" question. With every *weenie* word, the class became more out of control. Timmy saw my discomfort and he fed upon it like a hungry piranha. I had to think fast. The other children were waiting for my response, and I knew that my answer would set the tone for my entire stay in this classroom.

What was I supposed to say?

Discussion questions

1. What do you think Ms. King should say to Timmy? What are her choices? Defend your answer. How would your answer change if Timmy were 2 years old? Eight years old?

2. How should teachers handle other types of inappropriate language? How do you know what is inappropriate? Does everyone agree about what is inappropriate?

3. Do you think Ms. King should have stopped reading the story to speak to Timmy? What guidelines can you come up with about when to keep reading a story and when to stop for students' comments?

4. How do Lev Vygostky's thoughts about the role of social interaction in learning affect your views in this case? How about Jean Piaget's thoughts about the role of social interaction?

5. What planning can teachers do to minimize bathroom accidents such as the one in this case? What planning can be done to effectively cope with such accidents when they occur?

Giving It Some Thought

New Kid on the Block

Maria struggles with the question of how to integrate Tamara, a new student, into her class of 4- and 5-year-olds at the Head Start center. Tamara is often aggressive, damages materials, and throws tantrums when she doesn't get her way. How can Maria meet Tamara's socializing needs and handle the violent behavior?

It is 8:15 on a hot Tuesday morning in June. Jamal and Tamara are kicking each other under the table. I've already asked them twice to stop. I explained that they might spill their breakfasts if they continued. They stopped for a moment, but I knew that the fussing would soon begin again.

I hear a loud *BOOM!* Tamara has fallen out of her seat. Some children begin to laugh at her, and of course she doesn't like that. She feels humiliated and embarrassed.

Tamara has been in my class at our Head Start center for only two weeks. She just moved from another state and is 3 years old. She will not turn 4 for another month; however, she looks much older because she is tall. Tamara lives with both parents and has an older brother Gary who attends first grade in the public school nearby.

Tamara's parents are very concerned about her. At our first meeting they asked me for advice on handling her tantrums at home. Evidently her brother has always been a well-behaved, mild-mannered boy, so they haven't dealt with this type of behavior before.

Last year was my first year of teaching as an assistant in the 3-year-old class. This year I became the group teacher of the 4- and 5-year-olds. I didn't think the difference between the age groups would be significant; however, I was wrong. This year's class is more socially inclined during activities and play. The same children who last year played primarily by themselves now always play with a friend. The class has well-established play partners and groups. That's one reason why the transition into our class is so difficult for Tamara. She has helped me learn a great deal about the social needs of this older age group.

As I jump out of my chair, Tamara rises to her feet, crying furiously, and lashes out at the nearest person. She hits Tyrone because he is laughing. Yesterday she grabbed Billy because he took a block from her. I have tried moving where she sat within the classroom, thinking she had personality conflicts with the children she sat close to, but the hitting has continued, and I realize the solution is not that simple.

I know that Tamara needs time to adjust to the school setting because she has never gone to school before. She might miss the familiar surroundings of her previous home and want to go back. Perhaps she is acting out her anger and frustration. I can think of many reasons why Tamara feels angry and insecure, but I don't know what we can do to help her.

I realize we need to come up with a plan to help Tamara become part of the social group. How can we get the class to accept her and help her feel more comfortable? As I look over at Tamara standing next to the breakfast table, her angry face streaked with tears, I wonder what we can do.

Discussion questions

1. What do you think of Maria's analysis of the reasons for Tamara's anger? What other reasons can you list?

2. What do you know about the developmental differences between 3-, 4-, and 5-year-olds that can help you understand the circumstances in this case?

3. What advice would you give Maria for helping Tamara become part of the classroom community? What specific activities or strategies might she try?

4. How can Maria work with Tamara's parents to smooth her transition to school life? What specific actions can you suggest to involve Tamara's family?

5. What are some behaviors indicating that children are under stress that might not be as obvious as violent behavior? How can we help children cope with the stress in their lives?

What If I Don't Like Her?

Amy has one student in her kindergarten class who hasn't made any friends, doesn't get her work done, and lies to stay out of trouble. Amy is struggling with her own frustration over the fact that she doesn't really like this child and doesn't know how to respond to her.

"Oh, you poor thing. You've got Jane in your class this year? My heart goes out to you. I struggled with her all last year." "Hey, I'll bet she'll be pregnant before she reaches high school. If she even makes it to high school." "Yeah, well look at her mother. What can you expect?"

Here I am sitting in the teachers' lounge listening to my colleagues complain about their students again. I really should stop coming in here for lunch, but I find myself strangely needing to listen to others' problems and vent my frustration somehow.

This is my fourth year teaching kindergarten in a large suburb on the edge of a metropolitan area. The teaching is finally getting easier. I feel more confident in my planning and I know the curriculum well. But this year I'm facing a new challenge: I'm having a very difficult time liking Jane, one of my children.

Jane is repeating kindergarten and has encountered many problems in the eight weeks since the school year began. Her parents are divorced, and my impression is that she does not receive much support from her mother. She told me her mother thinks she's stupid. Jane's mother is the only parent who didn't make an appointment for a parent conference. I'm trying not to judge her on these impressions, but it's hard.

Jane does seem to have a good relationship with her father. She speaks very highly of him, and when she spends weekends with him, she glows with excitement the next day. She speaks often about her father reading to her, and she brings in books from her father's home to share with the class.

Jane wants attention and is willing to get it any way she can. For example, Jane is a very capable little girl, but she always asks for my help during independent worktime. At first I gave her the assistance she requested, but then I began to realize how easily she can do the work if she wants to.

One day in my frustration I said to her, "Jane, you can do this on your own. You're a very smart girl. You don't need my help!"

She responded with tears in her eyes, "No, I'm not smart. I'm stupid!" I tried to reassure her by saying, "But look at the good work you do. That proves that you are smart." I could tell that she was not convinced.

I tried to taper off the amount of time I assisted her, and all that accomplished was that she didn't do her work. I also tried to speak privately with her about why she misbehaves in class and doesn't finish her work. I tried using active listening to get her to open up, but she was unwilling to cooperate in the conversation. I didn't get anywhere with her.

Jane has not been able to develop friendships. She says nasty things to the other children, and she has already been involved in a few fights this year. She is the first to tattle on others but always denies it if something is said about her. This morning, out of the corner of my eye, I saw her take a granola bar out of Caroline's cubby. When I pulled it out of her pocket and questioned her about it, Jane lied right to my face, saying she brought it from home.

I believe I have shown the children in my class that I am fair. I explain that as long as they don't lie to me, I won't get mad. The children have responded very well to this. Jane, however, is extremely afraid to be in trouble.

I moved Jane's seat away from certain children at the request of their parents. They complained that Jane was saying bad things to their children and the children were getting upset. She now sits very close to my desk because it is the only place to keep her near the others yet limit her access to them. She is actually quite happy about it because she likes to be close to me.

In fact, Jane is always telling me how much she likes me and how nice I am. She is extremely attached to me. It makes me feel so guilty about my feelings toward her. It's as if she has no idea how annoyed I am with her.

I find myself getting angry about my reactions to her. I know deep down that this is a child in need who is reaching out for my help.

Every day I tell myself that I will try to like her more, but by the end of the day I always find myself annoyed with her. I spoke to her teacher from last year and I knew right away that she had an even harder time liking her than I do.

As I sit in the lounge listening to the teachers complain about kids in their classes, I become more and more uncomfortable. I don't want to sound like them, but what can I do about not liking Jane? I didn't think teachers ever felt this way!

Discussion questions

1. Do you think Amy's problem in not liking Jane is a common one? Explain.

2. What do you think is Amy's ethical responsibility in this case? What should she do about her feelings? How does applying the ethic of care in early childhood education relate to this case?

3. Why do you think children lie? What would you do about Jane's lying if you were in Amy's position?

4. Amy says that Jane feels she is stupid. What effect does such a self-perception have on Jane's learning and behavior? How would you try to change Jane's self-perception to be more positive?

5. Why do you think teachers complain so much about children? Is this unethical? Why or why not?

Superheroes Are Taking Over

Eunice's classroom is being overrun by the superhero play of her 4- and 5-year-olds. She can't decide whether to ban superhero play or look for a way to compromise without getting rid of it completely.

"Okay, get ready to shoot! The bad guys are gonna be here any minute!" shouts Daniel at the top of his lungs.

Jorge, carrying a long rectangular unit block over his shoulder, rushes over to Daniel. Together they point their block guns at Sammy and Manuel, who are crouched behind a block wall. "Eh-eh-eh-eh-eh-eh," come the staccato gun sounds as the four boys run full speed through the block area and crash into Eduardo's building. Eduardo begins to cry and rushes over to the art table where I am sitting.

As I comfort Eduardo I contemplate once more what to do about superhero play in our classroom. I truly love watching demonstrations of the creative imaginations of my 4- and 5-year-olds, and I appreciate the value of the learning that takes place in play. That's why I am torn over what to do about my "superheroes."

In the 17 years I've been teaching, I've seen the themes range from Star Wars and Masters of the Universe, to Ninja Turtles and Power Rangers, and right back to Star Wars again. The degree to which themes based on movies and TV shows dominate children's lives amazes me—lunch boxes, T-shirts, children's books, Halloween costumes. Such themes have taken over the children's imaginations.

As soon as choice time is announced, the boys (with an occasional appearance by Liliana, who is quite assertive herself) take command of the block area for their play scenarios. Roles are chosen with quite a bit of negotiation. Often no one wants to be the bad guys; either they remain purely in the realm of players' imaginations, or the girls playing quietly in the housekeeping area become unwitting targets.

Without redirection on my part, the play soon degenerates to a level of energy that just doesn't work in our small classroom. The yelling, running, and shooting beckon me urgently to the block area to calm things down.

I have known teachers who banned superhero play in their classrooms. It seems like a simple and final solution, although I imagine they must work hard at weeding out the seedlings of superhero play that continue to sprout, like the poison ivy I am battling in my yard. I recognize that the themes of superhero play resonate with my preschoolers in a way that is compelling and stimulating. They need to act out rituals of good versus evil. They need to become all-powerful and scare away the demons hiding deep below their consciousness. That's why I can't bring myself to outlaw superheroes; I understand too well the purpose that this kind of play serves.

On the other hand, the children playing at superhero themes do not use their imaginations to their fullest. The roles and characterizations of the superheroes are prescribed by television writers. The plots rarely vary, and there's little chance of gender equity appearing soon. The children in my class are certainly acting out the roles, but I know they are not writing the scripts.

I guess the biggest concern I have with superhero play is the violence. I have three children of my own and I have never encouraged gun play among them, limiting their weapons to water shooters and pretend pirate cannons. I've taught my children from an early age that guns are weapons that hurt and kill. I'm very uncomfortable with children pretending to shoot and kill each other, especially given the fact that they watch realistic violence on TV without seeming to bat an eye. Aren't we teaching

children that violence is okay? That the way to solve problems is to have more power and kill the other guy? How can such play scenarios possibly be healthy?

Some children in the classroom are bothered by the gun play and the superhero takeover. I have made a class rule that says no one can shoot at another person. This means of course that the shooting goes on, but aimed at imaginary targets. During the morning playtime I often hear complaints about boys who are not following the rules.

I'm also concerned about the domination of the block corner by the superhero band. It has created more gender segregation than I am comfortable with and has kept some children from the block area who would like to use it. Furthermore, the superheroes limit their own experiences by not visiting the art center, library corner, or other activity areas.

As I ponder this dilemma, I hear Daniel plotting new ways to annihilate the bad guys hiding under the doll blankets in the housekeeping corner. While Jorge searches for new weapons, I struggle to decide whether to intervene. It's only the first week in October, but I have to make changes in my classroom before it's too late. What should I do?

Discussion questions

1. What advice would you give Eunice about the superhero play in her classroom? What are all the options you can think of? What would the positive and negative results of each be?

2. Do you agree with Eunice that superhero play fulfills a need in her preschoolers' lives? What aspects of Erik Erikson's theory of psychosocial development can bring insights to this case?

3. Why do children segregate themselves by gender? What specific things can a teacher do to encourage gender equity in play?

4. What kind of rules do you think are appropriate for children's behavior in a preschool class? How would you enforce those rules? What do you know about classroom management that also affects children's behavior?

5. In your own experience with young children, what effects have you noticed television to have on their lives? What are the positive and negative aspects?

I Lost It!

Isabelle, a new teacher in a first-grade class, struggles daily with Randy's behavior until one day she loses her patience and punishes him. Now she wonders whether she did the right thing or if there was a better way to handle the situation.

When I was offered my first job in an urban school, I relaxed a little bit. I have spent most of my life in urban areas and I'm familiar with urban children and their needs. My student teaching experience had been in a public preschool class that was as perfect as I could imagine. I loved every day of it! I thought to myself happily, "What can really go wrong here?"

Well, little did I know.

My current problem started on the first day of the school year. When I walked into the classroom, I was surprised when the first thing I saw was Randy's little face smiling at me. Two years ago I completed a field experience in a local child care center that Randy attended. Now I was to face him again on my own in first grade!

What I know about Randy's background comes from teachers' information at both schools. Randy is an African American boy who had been adopted by a White gay man. His drug-addicted biological mother told Randy to his face that she didn't want him. Randy doesn't see her anymore. He also has two brothers from the same father who were adopted by different families.

The first few days of class everything went fine. Randy acted up sometimes, but every time I talked to him, he behaved well again. Randy has gradually become more defiant, annoying the other children and me. He rarely pays attention during group instruction, rocking back in his chair, pulling things out of his desk, and talking to his neighbor.

I've arranged the classroom with the desks in groups of four, but I've struggled with whether or not to separate Randy from his group. When we work on cooperative small-group activities, he is anything but cooperative! Randy always seems to be poking the child sitting next to him, teasing the other group members, knocking books off the desks, or refusing to do the job assigned to him.

Today started out as an especially bad day for Randy. He came in the door with a chip on his shoulder and it quickly got worse. Every time he started acting up, I took him out in the hallway to talk to him, just as my college professors had suggested.

This seemed to work until just before dismissal, when I saw Randy get right up in Joseph's face. Then Randy yelled at the top of his lungs, "I will f— you up, man. I'm gone f— up your mother if you don't shut up."

I could not believe my reaction when I heard those words coming out of Randy's mouth. All the years I spent in college learning how to talk and behave in different teaching situations were erased from my memory! I yelled at Randy at the top of my lungs, then grabbed his hand and practically dragged him out into the hall. Then I declared the punishment that momentarily appeased my anger: Tomorrow when the class begins a project making rainsticks, Randy would not be allowed to participate.

After I calmed down and thought it over, I went to Joyce, my mentor teacher, to ask her advice about what I had done. She shrugged and told me, "Don't worry, everything is going to be OK." But deep inside I knew that everything I had done was wrong.

I keep wondering how I could have handled the situation better and not humiliated Randy in front of the whole class. Now, of course, I'm stuck with the punishment I doled out.

What am I going to do tomorrow?

Discussion questions

1. In what other ways could Isabelle have handled the situation with Randy? Do you agree that she did something wrong? Why or why not?

2. Retell this case from Randy's point of view. What do you think are the reasons behind his behavior? Brainstorm as many as you can think of. Review Abraham Maslow's hierarchy of needs. How can this information help you understand Randy's behavior?

3. What specific actions can Isabelle take to help Randy become more prosocial?

4. Do you think Isabelle should carry out her punishment or give Randy a reprieve? What would the positive and negative consequences be of each decision?

5. What effect, if any, do Isabelle's previous association with Randy and her knowledge of his home life have on her treatment of him? What do you know about the effects of teacher expectations that could give Isabelle insight into this case?

Stopping the Bully

Mike is trying to find ways to increase the community spirit in his second-grade class and foster a democratic classroom while also stopping Ryan from teasing and bullying the other children.

Ryan was sitting at the art center looking over at Nikki's drawing. "That's not the way you draw a cat. That looks ugly," he said.

I was upset by Ryan's comment and looked over to see the effect it had on Nikki. She look discouraged.

"Don't worry about what he said, Nikki. Do you like the picture you've drawn? That's the important thing." Nikki nodded. "Then it doesn't matter if Ryan likes it or not."

I'm not sure whether this helped Nikki feel better.

I turned to Ryan and told him once again to consider other children's feelings before he speaks. He agreed.

Ryan always agrees, but he does the same thing repeatedly. This problem really bothers me because I believe that for a classroom to be democratic, children need to feel comfortable and free to socialize and communicate. Ryan's comments are often negative and seldom constructive.

Ryan also wants to be the first for everything. This morning when I asked the class a question, Ryan raised his hand and called out, "Me, me, me!" I ignored his outburst and called on Catherine.

Ryan jumped up and wouldn't let anyone hear Catherine speak. He pointed at her saying, "Na, na, na, na, na, you made a mistake."

I spoke to Ryan in a firm voice: "We have talked about this before, Ryan. You need to give someone else a chance to speak. You couldn't even hear Catherine, so you wouldn't know if she made a mistake."

Similar situations occur regularly. Ryan often teases children, and some of them get so upset they cry. I've never seen him physically hurt anyone, but he doesn't have to; his words are painful enough.

I have talked to some of the other second-grade teachers and to Ryan's teacher from last year, seeking advice. I've tried ignoring him, praising him when he is friendly, and isolating him when he is nasty; however, nothing seems to work.

Ryan is an only child and his parents have been good about supporting his schoolwork. I spoke to his parents to find out what he is like at home and to get a better feel for the family dynamics. I learned that they have very high expectations for Ryan. They often throw out his work if they feel it is not good enough. I tried to suggest that high expectations were important, but if they are unrealistic they could hurt Ryan's self-esteem, creativity, and confidence. I don't think they understood.

I asked Ryan's parents for suggestions to help Ryan be more kind and cooperative with the other children. They said that at home they send him to his room whenever he acts up and that maybe I could send him out to sit in the hall.

I have thought about this, but it doesn't fit in with what I want to accomplish. I'm trying to build community spirit and teach the children to be supportive of each other and understand the reasons behind our class rules. Banning Ryan from the room goes against my value system. But if I don't do something soon, the community spirit in the classroom will be completely gone.

Children can't learn in an environment in which they don't feel comfortable. But how am I going to build community spirit with Ryan's bullying?

Discussion questions

1. What advice do you have for Mike about getting Ryan to stop bullying? What do you think about the strategies he has tried so far? Why do you think they haven't been effective?

2. How can Mike work with Ryan's parents to come up with some new strategies?

3. How important is community spirit in early childhood classrooms? To what extent do you think it affects academic learning? Why?

4. How do children develop moral values? Should this process be left to parents, or should schools be concerned with moral development? How does culture affect moral values?

5. Compare the ideas of Lawrence Kohlberg, Carol Gilligan, and Mikhail Bakhtin about moral development in early childhood. How can these theories help Mike in making classroom decisions?

Resources for further reading

Areglado, R.J., R.C. Bradley, & P.S. Lane. 1996. *Learning for life: Creating class-rooms for self-directed learning*. Thousand Oaks, CA: Corwin.

This book promotes self-directed learning in which students begin to teach themselves based on knowledge of their own work habits, insights, and value systems. It is especially appropriate for primary grade teachers who want their children to have self-motivated, lifelong learning.

Berk, L.A., & A. Winsler. 1995. *Scaffolding children's learning: Vygotsky and early childhood education*. Research into Practice Series, vol. 7. Washington, DC: NAEYC.

This thorough volume presents Vygotsky's life and works, his approach to development compared to others' perspectives, and his views on the role of play, children with serious learning and behavior problems, and classroom applications.

Boyd, B.J. 1997. Teacher response to superhero play: To ban or not to ban? *Childhood Education: Infancy through Adolescence* 74 (1): 23–28.

Boyd gives an overview of play and aggression, discusses the developmental function of play, and argues against banning superhero play. She offers suggestions for more productive strategies in dealing with superhero play.

Buzzelli, C.A. 1995. The development of moral reflection in the early childhood classroom. *Contemporary Education* 66 (3): 143–45.

Buzzelli examines the sociocultural approach to moral reflection based on Vygotsky's and Bakhtin's work. This approach provides the rationale for engaging children in authentic, critical communication to develop self-regulation and moral reflection.

Carlsson-Paige, N., & D. Levin. 1990. *Who's calling the shots? How to respond effectively to children's fascination with war play and war toys*. Philadelphia: New Society.

Identifying the problems of high-tech war toys in combination with an increasingly violent attitude in society and in the media, the authors conclude that war play is an explosive mix that must be dealt with diplomatically instead of disallowed as forbidden fruit or shrugged off as "natural." They suggest several strategies to return creative control of play to children and to lessen the emphasis on violent content.

Cherry, C. 1983. *Please don't sit on the kids: Alternatives to punitive discipline*. Belmont, CA: Fearon.

This very practical book takes a hard look at the traditional idea that discipline equals punishment. Instead of humiliation and intimidation, Cherry offers a "magic list" of alternative approaches to developing social responsibility and self-respect. It is a good choice for beginning teachers seeking hands-on ideas to use in their classrooms.

Developmental Studies Center. 1996. *Ways we want our class to be: Class meetings that build commitment to kindness and learning*. Oakland, CA: Author.

This guide for class meetings comes from years of work in classrooms in the Child Development Project, a comprehensive school-change effort to help elementary schools become inclusive communities where students care about each other and about learning.

DeVries, R., & B. Zan. 1994. *Moral classrooms, moral children: Creating a constructivist atmosphere in early education.* New York: Teachers College Press.

The authors describe the theoretical foundation for focusing on social and moral development in the classroom. They offer advice for specific situations—conflict resolution, group time activities, cleanup, lunchtime, naptime, and handling the "difficult" child—as well as general aspects such as academics and the school atmosphere.

Dyson, A.H. 1997. *Writing superheroes: Contemporary childhood, popular culture, and classroom literacy.* New York: Teachers College Press.

Based on ethnographic study in an urban classroom of 7- to 9-year-olds, this book examines how popular culture affects young children. Through superhero stories of the children, Dyson presents a view of the complex interactions between young children's unofficial peer social world and the official school curriculum.

Fortis-Diaz, E. 1998. Just who are these "bad guys" anyway? An attempt at redirecting children's aggressive play. *Early Childhood Education Journal* 25 (4): 233–37.

Kindergarten children were observed for occurrences of aggression in their dramatic play and the circumstances surrounding them. Different strategies were implemented, resulting in a slight decline in the children's aggressive play.

Erikson, E.H. 1963. *Childhood and society.* New York: Norton.

This landmark work on the social significance of childhood has greatly influenced modern understanding of human development. Outlining eight states in emotional development, this book also explains a psychoanalytic perspective of early childhood. Included are case studies and anecdotes to illustrate the main ideas.

Gilligan, C. 1982. *In a different voice: Psychological theory and women's development.* Cambridge, MA: Harvard University Press.

Gilligan examines the way that women make moral decisions based on their desire to maintain relationships and sustain connections to others. She contrasts this with traditional moral reasoning theory in which universal principles are used for decisionmaking. This landmark volume stimulated many other writings about feminist moral theory and the ethic of care.

Maslow, A. 1999. *Toward a psychology of being.* 3d ed. New York: Wiley.

This book, outlining Maslow's theories of self-actualization and the hierarchy of needs, has become classic in educational psychology. Maslow identifies in an optimistic way the intrinsic values present in childhood and humanity, while offering insight into learners' motivations.

Paley, V. 1984. *Boys and girls: Superheroes in the doll corner.* Chicago: University of Chicago Press.

We listen in on children's conversations and stories as Paley uses her insightful observations to show us the children's gender differences during a year in her kindergarten classroom. Paley questions the way teachers reward stereotypical behavior that leads to domestic play by girls and adventurous fantasies by boys. She helps us examine our own biases and expectations for children.

Pollari, J., & J.R. Bullock. 1988. When children move: Some stresses and coping strategies. *Early Child Development and Care* 41: 113–21.

The authors identify factors that can contribute to stress in young children during family relocation. They offer strategies to smooth the transition.

Schaub, M. 1995. Cross-cultural dialogics: Bakhtinian theory and second language audience. Paper presented at the annual meeting of the Conference on Composition and Communication, Washington, D.C., March. ERIC, ED 385163.

This paper outlines the possible impact of Bakhtinian theory concept in English-as-a-second-language (ESL) instruction. Bakhtin's views on the culturally and politically embedded nature of language are ideal for discussions of cross-cultural communication and apply broadly to all ages, especially early childhood second-language learners.

4

Challenges of Children with Special Needs

Toddler Trouble

Sharon, a child care center director, wonders how she can better meet the needs of 2-year-old Marcus, who is a hemophiliac. Marcus's uncontrollable behavior endangers him and disrupts the class.

"Should I call his mother again?" the toddler teacher Glenda asked as 2-year-old Marcus struggled to free himself from her hold on his shoulders. Marcus tumbled on the floor by his naptime cot, falling over another toddler who had just gotten to sleep.

"Yes, I think you should. Marcus really needs her today."

Mrs. Jackson, Marcus's mother, came over from her office a few minutes later. She set Marcus on her lap in our large rocking chair. She gently stroked his back as she quietly read him a story. Slowly Marcus relaxed his little body, and about 20 minutes later he was asleep. Mrs. Jackson carefully laid him on his cot and slipped out the door back to work.

Marcus has been attending our corporate child care center since September. I'm the director of this center, which cares for 120 children, and I'm worried about Marcus. Marcus is a hemophiliac so we worry a great deal about his health and safety needs. We have to keep him safe from the normal bumps and bruises of children's lives.

But I'm also concerned about his behavior. Sometimes I shudder when I walk into the toddler room. He is often running around the room, pushing and shoving. He occasionally bites and hits the other children, and he screams at the top of his lungs whenever he is frustrated. Marcus seems to understand when we speak to him, but we usually can't understand what he is saying. He is still in diapers and it's a real challenge to get him to lie still long enough to change him.

I feel I should take some of the blame. I have been unable to keep a toddler teacher, thus disrupting the continuity in the classroom. I sometimes wonder if the stress of meeting Marcus's needs and handling his behavior has been part of the reason for the high turnover. It's now March, and Glenda the lead teacher is the fifth teacher since September.

Last month I tried to talk to Mrs. Jackson about having Marcus tested by a psychologist to rule out behavioral or neurological problems. We don't have the qualifications or training to make a diagnosis, but we have documented his behavior and feel he needs more evaluation. Mrs. Jackson responded that we were picking on Marcus because he's Black.

I was stunned by this statement because we are pleased with the ethnic and racial diversity we have in the center. Of our 10 toddlers, two are Asian, two African American, one Hispanic, and five Caucasian. Granted, most of the staff and children are Caucasian, but there are other children of color at the school. One of the five teachers who cycled through the toddler room was in fact African American.

Giving It Some Thought

I realize how difficult it must be for Mrs. Jackson and her husband. She started a new job in September, and because she works here in the same building as the center, the brunt of the responsibility for Marcus falls on her. She is very worried, understandably, about separating from Marcus because of his hemophilia. We call her immediately for any bump or scrape. Being called whenever Marcus is upset or out of control puts an added strain on her at her job. She regularly comes at naptime, as she did today. Some days Marcus won't calm down, so she takes him for a ride in her car until he falls asleep, then she brings him back to the center.

I feel we're not doing a good job meeting Marcus's needs or his mother's. And we have the other children in the classroom to consider as well. As I look at Marcus peacefully sleeping, I can't help thinking about the calm before the storm.

What can we do to better meet Marcus's special needs?

Discussion questions

1. How many suggestions can you make to Sharon about how she can better meet Marcus's needs?

2. Do you think the school and Marcus's parents are working well together? Why or why not? If not, what could be done to improve their relationship?

3. What considerations must the teachers make in protecting Marcus from physical harm?

4. What role do you think the high rate of teacher turnover has in this case? Why?

5. What can we learn from Loris Malaguzzi's ideas, illuminated in the Reggio Emilia approach, that would help in this case?

Can We Do This?

Debbie, a child care center director, finds herself enrolling Rebecca, a 3-year-old child with a physical disability, in the center. She wonders if this is really the best placement for Rebecca and whether the center can meet her needs.

A few years after becoming director of our child care center, I changed the enrollment forms. Our center has been fortunate enough to have a waiting list for many years, so when parents are interested in enrolling, they first fill out a form to be put on the waiting list.

Previously we had parents include a lot of information about their child on this form, but I found that unwittingly we were screening out kids we thought might be problems and not offering them a spot when one became available. Therefore, we came up with new forms for the waiting list that include only the child's age and parent's address, phone number, and so forth. We gave the family the full form to share information about their child only after they were offered a place at the center.

One early spring day, one of our parents came to tell me that her son Eric would be leaving the center. They were returning to China, their homeland, in another month. The following week I began the process of finding a 3-year-old child to fill Eric's space at the center.

The next child on the list was Rebecca Klein. I called and set up an appointment with her mother to visit the center and fill out the enrollment papers. Like many of the parents I offer spaces to, Rebecca's mom was delighted to be called. I would meet with her on Tuesday.

On Tuesday morning Eric's mom rushed into my office. She quickly explained that she had just found out that their plans for going back to China were postponed for another year. She wondered if there was any way that Eric could still stay at the center. I could see how distressed she was at the possibility that Eric would have to leave. I reassured her that Eric could stay and that we hadn't yet enrolled anyone else.

Of course, I didn't tell her that I had another parent on the way to enroll her child later that morning. I figured that that was my problem, and somehow I could make this new parent understand that emergencies happen and plans change.

When 11 o'clock rolled around, I saw a car pull up to our gate and a mother help her child out of the car. This must be Rebecca, I thought. Then I noticed that the mother was helping the child to struggle up our entranceway with a walker. I started to feel uneasy now about the problem that faced me.

I greeted Rebecca and her mom and lead them to my office. "I'm so glad you could come today," I began, feeling foolish. "Unfortunately, I have a problem that is not good news. The family of the child whose place we were offering to Rebecca has had a change in plans. They told me this morning that they will be staying here for another year. That means that I just don't have an opening that I can offer you right now."

Mrs. Klein nodded her head almost as if she expected this and said sadly, "That's what all the schools say when they see Rebecca."

I stumbled over my reply: "Oh no, it has nothing to do with Rebecca. I just don't have the space that I expected. I will be glad to keep Rebecca on the waiting list and let you know as soon as we get another opening. While you are here, why don't I give you a tour of the center so you can make sure it's the best place for her."

I felt like a heel as I showed them around the school, which was not easy with Rebecca's walker. Rebecca's mother seemed disappointed but not angry. I almost wished she had been madder at me. I felt terrible as I helped Rebecca into the car and said goodbye. I hoped she believed me.

Surprisingly, a few weeks later another family notified me that they would be moving and their child would be there only another month. As I called Rebecca's family again, I felt like I could redeem myself. But I was also worried about what I was getting us into.

This time both of Rebecca's parents came to the center to fill out the paperwork. We discussed at length the help Rebecca would need, what she could do on her own, and her strengths and weaknesses. For example, she was gifted intellectually and her fine motor skills were good, so she could draw and do art—and she even played the piano. Rebecca couldn't get into a chair, however, so she would have to lean against a table to work, which was actually good exercise for her legs. She could walk only with the walker, and sometimes she used a special wheelchair. Rebecca needed help to get down onto the floor at circle time, and she was completely dependent on an adult in the bathroom. Basically she needed a teacher with her all the time.

I began to be truly worried about our ability to meet Rebecca's needs.

"We are happy to have Rebecca join us, if you feel that this is the best place for her," I said to her parents, emphasizing *the best place*.

Mr. Klein answered quickly, "Oh, you are the only center willing to take her. The other centers in the area have told us she can't attend because she needs so much special attention. She has been enrolled in a preschool program for children with disabilities that requires an hour drive each way. Plus there are no other children with physical handicaps like Rebecca's. There are really no other children like her there. We want her to be included in a regular classroom and we have no other options."

Well, that was not the answer I had expected. How could this be true? No other center in our area would take her? I was surprised and embarrassed, and I was glad that Rebecca was enrolling here at our center.

I waved goodbye to the Kleins, telling them I would see them the following Monday. Then I turned around and walked back into the center, which was bustling with activity, children everywhere, excitement and friendship, caring and discovery. I wondered if we really could do this. I had to sit down and plan with the staff how we could welcome Rebecca into our community in the best way.

Discussion questions

1. Why do you think the Kleins had such a difficult time finding a center that would accept Rebecca?

2. What are some of the things that the teachers and director at this center need to consider in meeting Rebecca's needs? What planning will they have to do?

3. Should the teachers talk to the children about Rebecca's special needs before she comes? If so, what should they say?

4. What preschool services for children with special needs are available in your area? What are the most common disabilities that the children have?

5. Do you think Rebecca would be better off in a preschool with a special class for children with disabilities or in a regular child care center like this one? Why?

Why Is He in This Class?

*Sasha has a child in her class who she feels is develop-
mentally behind the other children. She wonders why the
director won't move him to a younger class and how she
can meet his needs and those of the other children at the
same time.*

Donald began attending my
class in January. By the second week I was asking myself, Why is
he in this class? He just doesn't seem to fit in with the rest of my 20
preschoolers, who will be going to kindergarten next year.

The first thing I noticed was that Donald seems to have a vision
problem. He turns his head toward or looks sideways at whoever
is talking to him. His pediatrician recommended that he go to an
eye doctor, but Donald hasn't seen one yet.

Donald is a bit taller than most of the other boys, and although
his bright red curls and dark brooding eyes make him look very
mature, he is far behind the other children in many developmental
areas. It is difficult to understand him when he talks, and we have
to give him directions at least three times before he seems to understand us. My assistant teacher thinks he may just be stubborn
and doesn't "want" to hear us, but I have a feeling there's more to
it than that.

Donald's large motor skills seem fine; he runs, jumps, and climbs
just like the other kids. However, his small motor skills are way
behind. He can't cut with scissors at all and he can hardly hold a
crayon. At lunch it's a real challenge for him to open food packages
or eat with a spoon without making a mess.

By January the other children had learned to recognize their own
names in print and many of the names of others. They could pick
them out on the mats they sit on at circle time, on the sign-up lists
for popular activity centers, and on each other's papers. Donald,

however, has difficulty recognizing or finding even the first letter in his name. Because of his problem with fine motor skills, he can't write his name legibly. During most of our whole class activities Donald seems lost.

Donald gets along fairly well with the other children, although he's quiet and doesn't usually take the initiative in social interactions. He tends to join a group of children, usually at table activities or art, and then follow their lead in whatever activity is under way. I don't remember ever seeing him in the dramatic play area or the blocks. I wonder if this relates to his verbal skills.

In fact it has been very easy for me to overlook Donald because he is so passive and causes so few problems. The other children lately seem to have recognized his difficulties. I have occasionally seen Joanne help him open his lunch items and Frankie write his name for him. They don't tease him, but they do seem to notice he's a little different from the other kids.

When I first noticed these problems in Donald, I went to the office to get more information from his file and to see what his parents had written about him on the registration papers. Unfortunately, our director was on a leave of absence for almost three months and had locked the files in her office. Unbelievable but true. I didn't feel comfortable asking his parents questions before I learned more about him, observed him more closely, and looked in his file.

Finally last week, our director returned and I got to look at Donald's registration papers. The thing that leaped out at me was the fact that he is so young. The other children in my class have been

Giving It Some Thought

turning 5 since November, so almost half of them are 5 already. Donald won't turn 5 until October, so he's almost a year younger than some of the others. Other than that I found nothing unusual in his file.

I suggested to the director that, given his age and developmental level, Donald might do much better in the younger class in our center. She wouldn't even consider this alternative because there was no space for another child in that room, and transferring Donald would make my room one child short.

My first plan, of course, is to set up a time to meet with Donald's parents to get more information from them and share my observations. I wonder if I should suggest to them that Donald would be better in the classroom with younger children who are similar to him in their needs, skills, and understanding. Perhaps his parents could speak to the director; she might listen to them. Wouldn't this be better for Donald?

Discussion questions

1. Do you think Donald would be better off in the younger class? List as many advantages and disadvantages as possible before you reach a decision. How do Maria Montessori's ideas about multiage grouping affect your thinking in this case?

2. If you were meeting with Donald's parents, what questions would you ask them? What other information would you want to have? How would you share with them the information you have about Donald?

3. If Donald remains in this classroom, what accommodations can Sasha make to meet Donald's needs? What specific things should she consider?

4. Do you think that Donald's behavior, as Sasha describes it, shows developmental problems? Be specific.

5. How do critics of traditionally defined child development and developmentally appropriate practice, such as Jonathan Silin, give us insight into viewing this case from other perspectives? For example, what role might culture play in looking at Donald's developmental progress? Is looking through the lens of developmental psychology the only way to view a child?

Outburst Annie

Kevin tries hard to meet the needs of Annie, a perceptually impaired girl in his overcrowded kindergarten class, but he wonders if this placement is best for Annie.

From my first days of teaching kindergarten this year, I heard horror stories about Annie and all her problems both in school and at home.

Annie is a special child. She was a crack baby who has recently been removed from her mother's custody because of her mother's drug addiction and her physical abuse of her children. She is classified as *perceptually impaired* and was mainstreamed into my urban kindergarten classroom with 27 other children.

In class Annie is unable to sit still for more than a few minutes. She seems to lack the social skills necessary to form friendships with her peers. She is 5 years old and she makes it known repeatedly that she has no friends, she is stupid, and no one loves her.

On the second day of school Annie broke into tears. "Mr. Moore," she said, "you're the only one who loves me." Can you imagine being 5 and truly believing a total stranger is the only one who loves you?

I said, "Annie, I know your mommy loves you even though you don't think so. So does your grandma."

"No," she quickly remarked, "Mommy doesn't care about anybody but herself. Grandma told me so. Grandma says if I don't behave, Mommy will take me away from her. I try to be good, I really do. It's not my fault. I can't help it." She sobbed uncontrollably as she banged her head and fists on the table.

As time progresses, I lose more and more control of Annie. She rarely joins in activities with the rest of the class. She spends a great deal of time just wandering around, and she plays with the materials in our learning centers at inappropriate times. She cannot sit still in her seat and she's very impulsive. She frequently grabs things from other children or demands my attention when I am working with a small group or talking to the whole class.

Annie's achievement level is way below most of the other children's, so she is often frustrated by our curriculum. Many times she can't complete activities without some guidance from me. I have tried rearranging the class schedule and planning more physically active projects for Annie. I have also decided to be more firm in setting limits on her behavior.

Today we had just returned from our bathroom break down the hall, and I was quieting the class down so I could give them directions for the science activity I had planned. Just when I had everyone's undivided attention, Annie jumped up from her seat and threw herself onto me.

"I love you, Mr. Moore," she said as she nearly squeezed all the air out of me.

"Annie, Annie," I calmly replied. "Annie, please let go of me. You're hurting me."

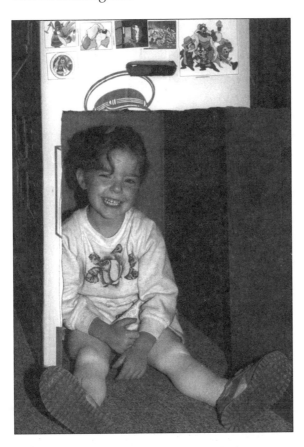

"Oh no, I'm not. I'm just loving you, that's all. You're my best friend, right?" She stared up at me, fluttering her long brown eyelashes, and continued to give me her best attempt at a bear hug.

The class was in an uproar of laughter and I had a 5-year-old wrapped tightly around my body. How can I possibly teach with such disruptions?

Wouldn't Annie be better off in a special education class where she could get the attention she needs? Is it really in her best interest to be mainstreamed here in my class with 27 other children and no teacher assistant? More important, how can I tell Annie to stop when all she is trying to do is return the love I give her?

Discussion questions

1. What can Mr. Moore do to better meet Annie's needs in his kindergarten class? Name all the strategies you can think of.

2. At what point (if any) do you think a child with special needs is better off in a more restrictive setting than being mainstreamed or participating in an inclusive setting?

3. What effect does class size have on classroom management and children's behavior? What strategies can be used to teach a large class such as this?

4. What other information would you want to know about Annie to help meet her needs? What sources are available for getting this information?

5. What are the procedures in your state and your school for identifying children with special needs and determining appropriate placements for them?

Giving It Some Thought

Learning Disabilities or Differences?

Luisa struggles with how to increase Isaac's achievement in first grade when Isaac and the other adults in his life have low expectations for him because of his learning disability. She questions whether Isaac actually has a disability or just has strengths in other areas.

Isaac looks up at me with frustration and says, "I'm doing the best I can."

I reply with encouragement, "I know you are. Let's try again."

Isaac has brought me his journal and I am helping him sound out one of the words he can't read, even though he wrote it. This is Isaac's second year in first grade, and I'm trying to make sure he moves on to second grade next year. He has been classified as learning disabled, and because our district believes strongly in inclusion, he is in a regular classroom with me and 22 other children from our affluent suburban area.

Sometimes I wonder if Isaac hasn't already internalized the idea that he doesn't have to learn what the other kids are learning or have high expectations for himself. He often repeats the phrase "I'm doing my best," and I have heard his parents say to him many times that he only has to do the best he can. What worries me is what he thinks "the best he can" really means.

I truly wish that I had been Isaac's teacher last year instead of this year. I fantasize that I could have "saved" him from repeating first grade and being classified. He scored at almost the lowest possible level on last year's standardized test, partly because he couldn't read any of the questions.

To be honest, I'm not really sure this whole idea of having a learning disability makes any sense. If Isaac has an average intelligence level and yet isn't learning in school, doesn't that mean it's a problem in the learning environment, not in the child? I like to think of him as *teaching disabled* rather than learning disabled.

It seems to me that Isaac now has a label that excuses his parents and former teachers from taking any responsibility for his not learning. Having a medical-sounding term makes them feel more comfortable because it confirms that the problem is inside him, not them.

I think intelligence is too narrowly defined in our school. When I look at Isaac, I see his strengths, not his weaknesses. For example, Isaac is very artistic. He draws pages of complex, detailed designs of airplanes, boats, and starships. He also sings like an angel. Coming and going from class and in between activities, Isaac usually sings softly some of the folk songs he has learned at home. His voice is beautiful, right on pitch.

Isaac is also well coordinated and seems to be quite athletic. I watched him play soccer outside with the other children yesterday, and I was surprised at how good he is. How can he master these complex skills if he is learning disabled?

My problem now is that Isaac sees himself as learning disabled. This not only decreases his motivation to try new things, but I think it also allows him to set his personal standards lower so he doesn't have to try very hard.

How am I ever going to get Isaac through first grade if I can't get him and the other adults in his world to believe he can do it?

Discussion questions

1. What do you think of Luisa's assertion that Isaac is teaching disabled rather than learning disabled? Do you agree or disagree? Why?

2. Have you ever known any children who were weak in academic subjects but excelled in other areas such as drawing or sports? How do you explain that in terms of learning ability?

3. How can you use Howard Gardner's theory of multiple intelligences to analyze this case?

4. What role do you think teacher and parent expectations play in learning? Can you give any personal examples?

5. What advice can you give Luisa? How can she build up Isaac's belief that he can succeed? How many ideas can you come up with?

"Hey, Stupid!"

Mrs. Jenkins is worried about the teasing that Frankie, who has a developmental delay, endures from the other children in their mixed-age, kindergarten-to-second-grade class.

"Hey, stupid! Why don't you try kicking the ball for a change!" Joey yelled at Frankie.

I quickly decided it was time to intervene. "Joey, we do not speak to each other like that! I won't have it. Either change your attitude or you will not play the game."

"But he doesn't even know how to play right, Mrs. Jenkins!" Joey whined.

"Give him a chance. Frankie is part of this team and he's doing fine." I tried to smooth things over. I felt like I was losing the battle for Frankie, however. Every day, in one form or another this teasing is played out.

Frankie is a member of our small mixed-age class of kindergartners through second-graders. At 8 years he is one of the older children, but he has a developmental delay that makes it hard for him to do what the other kids do. Frankie is awkward in his movements, has a streak of white in his dark black hair, and often drools.

We live in a rural area with very few children, so we have to combine classes. There are no special education classes at our school because it is so small, so Frankie spends all his time in our class. I worry a lot about Frankie because I have such a hard time getting the other children to accept him. His academic work is a year or two behind that of other kids his age, but in our multiage classroom this is not too noticeable. His physical appearance and social skills account for the way the other children treat him.

I often hear Frankie's classmates teasing him, especially calling him names like "stupid" or "retard." This usually happens when I am not directly in charge of the group, like at lunchtime or recess when the children play kickball. When we have center time, I've noticed the kids subtly trying to avoid working with Frankie. Sometimes they will even tell him to go away. Occasionally Samantha and Elena watch over him in a very nurturing way, but none of the children treats him like a friend.

Sometimes when I pick up the kids from recess, I stand at the side of the playground and watch the dynamics of the group, hoping to get an insight into handling the problem. When the kids start calling Frankie names, he looks blankly at the other children as if nothing has really registered. This seems to encourage the kids to continue their harassment, almost as if they are trying to see how far they can go. Eventually Frankie breaks into tears, and then the children seem genuinely remorseful and they back off. Why do they always take it to extremes?

This is a small community, so everyone knows everyone else. This group of children has been together since they started school. Each year one-third of them moves on to the upper-grade class. The combination of kids I have this year seems to make the situation worse. The children are homogeneous in many ways. They are all White, so we don't have racial differences, and the kids all come from low- to moderate-income families.

I wonder if it is human nature for children to find something different to tease each other about. I also wonder how much of this might be encouraged by the parents of the kids in my class. I know

Giving It Some Thought

many of the parents personally and they can be very discriminatory. It wouldn't surprise me if some of the children hear their parents say nasty things about Frankie at home.

I feel that this is a critical time for Frankie's self-esteem. I want to create a more comfortable environment for him, and I want the other children to learn tolerance and acceptance of people who are not like themselves. Isn't this the most important thing we can teach young children? But what am I doing wrong?

Discussion questions

1. What, if anything, do you think Mrs. Jenkins is doing wrong? Is teasing an inevitable part of childhood, or should we expect children to be more tolerant?

2. What advice would you give Mrs. Jenkins? What specific suggestions can you make for helping her foster tolerance, acceptance, and understanding?

3. What suggestions can you come up with for working with the families at this school to help promote tolerance?

4. Do you think a mixed-age class has any effect on the success of inclusion? In what ways?

5. What, if anything, can teachers do about the behavior of their classes when the children are not directly under their supervision, such as at lunchtime or recess?

The Cartwheel Kid

Carol has difficulty managing her second-grade class due to the disruptions caused by George, a child with attention deficit hyperactivity disorder. How can she plan activities that meet the individual needs of the class and best help George?

George was standing near his desk, kicking his legs in the air, spinning around, and flailing his arms everywhere. I tried desperately to continue my math lesson on borrowing and subtraction. As I tried my best to raise my voice over George's singing, the rest of the second-graders tried their hardest to listen.

"I think the people on that side of the room could see the board a lot better if you sat down, George," I said gently.

"Yeah, George, sit down!" cried a classmate.

"Please!" begged another.

I was well aware that George was not focused on the lesson, so I gave him three options: join the class

Giving It Some Thought

in the math lesson, read a book, or write in his journal. He chose to read a book. "Great," I thought, "that will keep him quiet." George proceeded to read the book aloud. Now I was about to lose my mind. I asked him nicely to please read to himself.

"I am reading to myself!" he answered.

"Silently!" I answered back with a bit too much anger creeping into my voice.

He put the book down and continued his song-and-dance routine. The class rolled their eyes at him and tried to concentrate on math.

George has been diagnosed as having attention deficit hyperactivity disorder (ADHD). He is impaired neurologically as a result of an extremely high level of lead in his blood. He has little control over his words or actions. If he feels like doing a cartwheel in the middle of a lesson, he's going to do one—and he has done this.

During the day he doesn't get any work accomplished. He openly admits that his mother does his homework for him and lets him write the answers. In the afternoon he goes to basic skills, and the second he walks out of our door, the class lets out a sigh of relief.

I struggle daily to get through the day's lessons. Having taught for only a few years, I am having trouble accepting that there is nothing I can do if George refuses to work. I have tried giving him options and empowering him by letting him choose an activity with which he feels comfortable. However, even if he is doing something he loves—drawing, for example—he is still disruptive. I am fully aware that it is not his fault, and my heart breaks every time one of his friends asks him to be quiet. But what can I do?

George's mother heard the diagnosis straight from the doctor's mouth, but she refuses to sign the papers allowing him to be referred to the child study team. She feels that labeling him will do more harm than good and that he is better off in a regular classroom. She told me that if he gets a special ed classification, then teachers' expectations will be lower and he will achieve less.

I can see her point, but I feel that because she refuses to sign, George will never get the attention he needs. Not only is he not learning, but he is hindering his classmates' learning as well. The singing and dancing today is low-key compared with the shouting matches and chair throwing that often occur. His mother also refuses to consider medication to help George control his impulses and concentrate better. I have taught children who showed great improvement with medication, but I can't convince her to try it.

I am having the life drained out of me. Furthermore, I feel that I am not doing my job to the best of my ability because one child gets most of my attention. George's psychologist advises that I simply ignore him. How can I ignore his erratic behavior when 30 other 8-year-olds are trying to learn? How can I get through this so that everyone, including George, gets the most out of the school year?

Discussion questions

1. What are the referral procedures for students being considered for the special education program in your school or area? What are the requirements? If you were to have a conference with George's mother, what would you say? How would you ask her to give permission for George to be tested? Do you think parents should have the right to refuse to have their child evaluated or classified?

2. What role, if any, do classroom management and curriculum play in contributing to George's difficulties? What do you know about classroom management that could help Carol to meet George's needs while still maintaining an effective learning environment?

3. What courses of action can Carol choose in helping George socially, emotionally, and academically? Check with someone with a background in special education for his or her perspective on this case.

4. How well prepared are you to work with children with special needs in your classroom? What further knowledge or skills do you feel you need?

5. How do you feel about medicating children who have been diagnosed with ADHD? What are the pros and cons? How should this decision be made?

Resources for further reading

Armstrong, T. 1987. *In their own way*. New York: Putnam.

Armstrong builds on Howard Gardner's theory of multiple intelligences to show that cultural values put more importance on some forms of intelligence than on others, causing some children to experience less success in schools. He questions the concept of disabled learners, seeing children with learning disablities as casualties of the boredom resulting from poor instruction. He offers inspirational activities and resources to encourage the development of many intelligences.

Chandler, P. 1994. *A place for me: Including children with special needs in early care and education settings*. Washington, DC: NAEYC.

This book encourages teachers and caregivers to include children with special needs in their settings, and it offers practical advice to help them meet the challenges of making inclusion work.

Chattin-McNichols, J. 1992. *The Montessori controversy*. Albany, NY: Delmar.

This excellent review of the strengths and weaknesses of the Montessori method provides detailed information about the specifics of the method, the misconceptions, the history of Montessori education, and the effects of Montessori school experience.

Favazza, P.C. 1998. Preparing for children with disabilities in early childhood classrooms. *Early Childhood Education Journal* 25 (4): 255–58.

This article focuses on attitudes, formed at a very early age, toward individuals with disabilities. It discusses ways to promote acceptance by typically developing children of children with disabilities in their primary social group.

Finlan, T.G. 1994. *Learning disability: The imaginary disease*. Westport, CT: Bergin & Garvey.

This controversial book proposes that educational practices such as labeling, testing, and segregation by achievement level, as well as poor instruction, have caused children to be relegated to the ranks of the learning disabled. The author reaffirms the theme that all children are capable of learning and offers suggestions especially to parents on how to avoid having their children labeled and how to take control of their children's educational experiences.

Gardner, H. 1993. *Multiple intelligences: The theory into practice*. New York: Basic Books.

Gardner describes the diverse educational applications of multiple intelligences (MI) theory that have been developed in the 10 years following publication of *Frames of Mind*. This book includes an overview of the theory, discussion about educating the intelligences, assessment issues, and future directions for MI theory.

Goldstein, L.S. 1998. More than gentle smiles and warm hugs: Applying the ethic of care to early childhood education. *Journal of Research in Childhood Education* 12 (2): 244–61.

The author takes us on a journey into a primary-grade classroom to see how the ethic of care is applied in children's daily experiences. Goldstein also presents a clear overview of feminist moral theory and provoking conclusions about her research in this classroom.

Honig, A.S. 1997. Creating integrated environments for young children with special needs. *Early Childhood Education Journal* 25 (2): 93–100.

This articles shares practical ideas for teachers on meeting the challenge of inclusion, addressing the needs of the whole group, and ensuring the comfort and learning of all children in an integrated setting.

Kohn, A. 1998. Suffer the restless children: Unsettling questions about the ADHD label. In *What to look for in a classroom . . . and other essays,* 111–34. San Francisco: Jossey-Bass.

This provocative chapter takes a critical look at the history and abuses of labeling children with ADHD and prescribing Ritalin as a treatment.

Silin, J.G. 1987. The early childhood educator's knowledge base: A reconsideration. In *Current topics in early childhood education, volume 7,* ed. L.G. Katz. Norwood, NJ: Ablex.

Silin's essay questions how and why early childhood educators have come to rely on a psychological perspective. Limitations of the psychological perspective are explored through a brief analysis of Jean Piaget's work. Conclusions deal with the nature of appropriate knowledge for the young, the basis for the early childhood educator's professional expertise, and future directions in how early educators might think about themselves, their work, and the children they teach.

Stafford, S.H., & V.P. Green. 1996. Preschool integration: Strategies for teachers. *Childhood Education: Infancy through Adolescence* 72 (4): 214–18.

This article offers an overview of terminology related to integration and strategies to include in an integration model for programs.

Wolery, M., & J.S. Wilbers, eds. 1994. *Including children with special needs in early childhood programs.* Washington, DC: NAEYC.

A thoughtful overview of the challenges and opportunities of inclusion, this volume bridges research and practice.

5

Challenges of Stress in Children's Lives

Helping Jared to Separate

Kim is exhausted from dealing with the separation problems that 2-year-old Jared is experiencing. Every morning Jared ends up kicking and screaming when his mother leaves. Kim wonders how she can ease these transitions.

Jared was screaming and kicking me as I held him, trying to be gentle. When his mother waved goodbye, tears came to her eyes. She had already been at the center for 10 minutes trying to get Jared to calm down. Finally I gently peeled Jared off her legs so she could go to work. She turned away quickly, and we watched her walk down the path.

After a few more minutes of struggling, Jared gradually started to relax. He was still crying hard, so I held him and took him over to the library corner.

We sat down in the beanbag chair, I gave his nose a quick wipe, and I opened a book that I know Jared loves. By the end of the book, his cries were down to a whimper. One more nose wipe, and I asked

Jared if he wanted to read another book. He nodded yes and picked one out. By the end of this book, the tears had stopped.

I got up and put Jared on his feet. I needed to check on a few of the other children. As much as I wanted to, I couldn't cuddle with Jared all morning. There are 12 toddlers in our room with my assistant teacher Carly and me.

Jared joined us two months ago. During the first few weeks, his mom couldn't leave him at all. Sometimes

I think she was more upset about the separation than Jared was. But her work obligations demanded that she leave, so for the last couple of weeks we have gone through this screaming and crying each morning.

"Okay, Jared, let's put your coat here in your cubby," I said.

"No!" he replied, and the tears started to well up in his eyes.

"Jared, you can't wear your coat all day—it's not good for you. You'll be too hot in here."

I'd repeated this same line every day for a week. At first we forced Jared to take his coat off, but he cried and whimpered the whole day. For some reason wearing his coat helps him separate from his mother more easily. The last few days we've let him keep it on, but it just doesn't seem right to me. Won't he be cold when we go outside later? Will this make him sick?

"Come on, Jared, please hang up your coat. You can put it on again when you go outside in a little while."

"No!" Jared wasn't giving in. I decided it wasn't worth the fight.

Seeing Jared, some of the other kids wanted to wear their coats inside. I told them no. I guess they will just have to understand that Jared needs his coat right now.

In the meantime I was exhausted, and I'd only been at work for an hour. This daily ritual of helping Jared to separate from his mother was wearing me out. At first I thought I could handle it for a few days or so, but now it's been a few weeks and I can't tell if it's any better.

Jared, his mother, and I are all emotionally drained. There must be a better way. What can we do?

Discussion questions

1. Why do you think Jared and his mother are having difficulty separating? Why do you think some children have more difficulty separating than others?

2. What suggestions can you make that Kim and Jared's mother might try?

3. Should Kim let Jared continue to wear his coat? Why or why not? Can you make other suggestions?

4. Do you think it is appropriate to allow some children to do things in class because they have special needs, but not others? What would you tell the other children who also want to wear their coats because they see Jared wearing his?

5. Retell this case from Jared's mother's perspective. What can you learn from this perspective that will help Kim decide what to do?

Should I Report This or Not?

Neela, an assistant teacher in a child care center, notices a suspicious-looking bruise on 3-year-old Christy's leg. She wants to report suspected child abuse, but her director doesn't want to upset the parent, and she tells the lead teacher Darlene not to report it.

Darlene and I have worried about Christy for a while now, but today we faced our concerns head-on. Christy is a precious little 3-year-old with blonde curly hair, big blue eyes, and a freckled nose. She lives with her single mom, who is a friend of Cheryl's, another assistant teacher at the center. From Cheryl we learned that Christy's mother has had a string of boyfriends who come and go. Christy has never known her father.

When Christy first started at the center, her mom dropped her off and she happily joined our class. She adjusted well throughout the day and got along well with the other children. We were surprised then that she acted so differently when Carl, her mom's boyfriend, came to pick her up. She started to whine and fuss and grabbed onto Cheryl's legs and refused to leave. Unfortunately, Christy's mom had given written permission for Carl to pick her up, so we had to let her go with him. The next day we mentioned this incident to Christy's mother, but she reassured us that Christy just needed more time to adjust to the new setting.

Over the months that followed, however, we saw a pattern develop. Christy would show distress whenever Carl came to pick her up. Christy told us that she doesn't like it when Carl stays at her house because then she doesn't get to sleep in her mom's bed with her.

Christy's anger also came out in her play. Almost every day she would head over to the doll corner as soon as playtime started. She would choose a doll or stuffed animal, yell at the toy, scold it, and spank it. She often called the doll "Carl" while she did this.

Christy's best friend Marlene would join her in the doll corner and quietly watch Christy go through this routine. Then the two of them happily played other themes. It seemed to us that Marlene knew intuitively that Christy needed to get this out of her system each day.

Today Christy was dropped off by her mom, and she had a pretty typical morning. At naptime Christy called me over to rub her back. The spring weather was warm enough today that most of the children were wearing shorts or sundresses like Christy's. As she rolled over on her belly to get comfortable, I couldn't miss seeing the glaring purple bruise on her left thigh. It was practically a perfect imprint of a large hand. I felt sick in my stomach. I waited until Christy fell asleep, then I called Darlene over and showed her the bruise. The look on her face confirmed my fears.

"We have to call the department of youth and family services right away. This is clearly child abuse, just like we learned in the child abuse workshop," Darlene proclaimed.

"I agree. Let's talk to Brenda to see who we're supposed call." Darlene went to get Brenda, our director. They both returned, and Brenda took a look at Christy's thigh. She agreed that it looked suspicious, but she was hesitant to act.

"We need to talk to Christy and find out what happened before we jump to conclusions," Brenda warned.

After nap we calmly asked Christy how she got the bruise. Each of us, including Cheryl, got a different answer—she fell down, she bumped into something, she fell off the bed. In the late afternoon Darlene and I again approached Brenda. "We really think that we should call youth services about this. We have to try to help Christy!" I said to Brenda.

Brenda seemed upset. "No, wait a minute. You don't have to call anyone. This is my problem to handle, not yours. I need to talk to Christy's mom first. We'd never stay in business if I called youth services every time a child had a bruise."

We were both surprised by Brenda's reaction, but we didn't argue with her. After Christy's mother came to pick her up, Brenda came to see us again. "Christy's mother is very upset by your accusations. She claims that Christy got that bruise here at school, going down the slide. I will continue to keep an eye on the problem so you two don't have to worry about it anymore." Brenda turned and left. Darlene and I were in a state of disbelief.

"Don't worry about it anymore? How can we do that? Right there in our staff handbook it explains that we are legally obligated to report suspected child abuse," I said.

"Yeah, but Brenda made it clear that this would hurt the school's reputation and she could lose enrollment. She doesn't want us to do anything that gets the parents upset. I just don't want to go against Brenda. I'm not going to put my job on the line!" Darlene said.

"But we are legally obligated. And besides, think about Christy. We have to do something," I tried to convince her.

"Well, you go ahead then. But I'm not going against what my boss wants me to do. Leave me out of it." Darlene picked up her coat and headed for the door.

I stared after her as the door closed. What should I do now?

Discussion questions

1. What are the regulations for reporting suspected child abuse in your state? What are your legal responsibilities as a teacher?

2. What are teachers' ethical responsibilities in a case like this? What do you think Neela should do? Should she report this incident or not?

3. What are some of the signs of child abuse to be aware of? Where can you get more resources about detecting child abuse? What other professionals are available to help?

4. If you observed a child acting out abusive situations during play, would you intervene or let the child continue? Why or why not?

5. In addition to support from social service agencies or psychologists, what classroom decisions can help a child who has been abused? What can we as teachers do to help ease this kind of stress in a child's life?

How Much Touching?

*Robert is trying to determine how he can give his kin-
dergarten children the love and caring they need without touching them. He wonders where to draw the line
between appropriate and inappropriate touches.*

We were coming in from
the playground when Chantal slipped on the gravel walk and
skinned her knee. She burst into tears as I hurried over to help her.
As she got up, Chantal hugged me tight around the legs. I gave her
a hug back and said, "Are you okay? Let's go inside and find a ban-
dage for that knee."

I let go of Chantal and unwrapped her arms from around my legs.
I knew she was in pain and upset, but I am very concerned about
people's perception of how I touch the children. Even this brief hug
made me uncomfortable. I know this is a problem for all teachers,
but I have to be especially careful because I'm male.

You wouldn't believe how many times I think about this and how
it affects my relationship with the children. Many of the children
give me a quick hug on the way home each day, and I think they
really need that. But I worry about how easily that can be misinter-
preted by others. The children always used to sit on my lap as we
read books in the library corner. It was a great way to bond with
the children and encourage them to develop a love of reading. Now
I have the children sit next to me. Sometimes I wonder if even that
could lead to problems.

Yesterday Francine came out of the bathroom and couldn't get
the buttons done up on her pants. "Why don't you see if Caroline
can help you? She's an expert with buttons!" I joked, trying to find
a way out of helping her in an awkward situation.

I have a great relationship with the parents in this class. Many of
the children don't have a father in the house, and their mothers often

tell me they are really glad that the children have a male role model now. A lot of these kids have some difficult life situations and are starved for love and attention.

My principal is very supportive and has let me keep my kindergarten assignment for the last 10 years. It is definitely my favorite age group! I love the creative spontaneity of children at this age, and I feel I can really make a difference in their lives.

I believe that young children's social and emotional development is as important as their intellectual development. They need to feel loved and cared for in a warm, encouraging environment. It's hard to show kids I care about them when I am always worried about whether my actions will be seen as inappropriate.

It's sad to me that our society has gotten to the point where we cannot trust adults to behave appropriately around children. And I certainly don't blame parents for being worried. I have two daughters of my own and I can't stand the thought of some creepy teacher touching them in inappropriate ways.

I find it difficult to know where to draw the line. All the teachers in our school are aware of the need to be careful in what they do. Some of the warm, comforting gestures that the women teachers make would not be appropriate for me to make. My friends on the faculty here warn me that I have to protect myself and I just shouldn't touch the kids at all.

How can I be a good kindergarten teacher and never touch the kids? How about helping a child get on her coat? Holding a child who is angry and trying to hit someone? Leaning over a child to look at her writing? Where do I draw the line? How much touching is too much?

Discussion questions

1. Where do you think Robert should draw the line? What guidelines should teachers use to decide what touching is appropriate?

2. How important is touching for young children's social and emotional development? Why?

3. How does the age of the children in Robert's class affect this case? How would you feel if the children were 2 years old? Ten years old? Fourteen years old?

4. Why do you think there are not more men working in early childhood education? Brainstorm this question and come up with as many reasons as you can.

5. If Robert decides that he should not touch the children at all, how can he still meet the needs of the children in his class? What compromises would you suggest?

Inappropriate Sexual Behavior

Lynn wonders how she can stop 4-year-old Alex's inappropriate sex play. How can she handle Alex's emotional needs while also protecting the other children in the class?

Did I hear what I think I heard? I moved closer to the dramatic play corner so I could listen to what Alex was saying.

"Come on, you want to see my pee-pee?" Alex started to undo his pants as Maggie and Imani looked at him uncomfortably. I could tell that even at 4 years, they knew something about this was not right.

"Alex, I need to talk to you. Come over here for a minute, please."

Alex jerked his head around and sheepishly walked away from the girls, heading over to the block area.

"Alex, I need to talk to you," I repeated.

He finally came over, and I explained that that kind of behavior was not okay and that he should leave the girls alone. He half listened, then escaped to the blocks.

Alex had been physically and sexually abused by his father, who is now in jail on drug charges. His father still has visitation rights, even in jail, and he sees Alex every other week. Alex is living now with his mother, aunt, two brothers, and two cousins.

It breaks my heart to think about what he has gone through in his short life. He is often angry and very impulsive. It is hard to predict how he will act in any given situation. And he is somewhat obsessed with the girls in the class. He always wants to play in the dramatic play area with them, and he makes me nervous. I find myself watching him carefully all the time.

I think Alex knows he is being watched, and he must feel that I don't trust him. And the reality is, I *don't* trust him. In the past, I have found him with his pants off, and he says things to the girls that only adults should say to each other. He has clearly heard this sex talk at home many, many times. One day I heard him trying to convince the girls to take off their clothes. I was so upset that I yelled at him and sent him to sit by himself in the other part of the room for a while.

Some of the parents have mentioned that they are concerned about Alex being in this class. He has a government-subsidized spot at our center, and frankly I think this is a much better daytime environment for him than home. Some of the children pay no attention to Alex or the things he says, while others seem fascinated by him. Maybe they are intrigued by the false sense of maturity he conveys.

I just don't know what to do to help Alex stop his inappropriate behavior. I never thought I would run into this kind of problem. After all, these kids are only 3 and 4 years old. I know I have to send him a clear message that this is unacceptable. Should I use stronger punishments? Should I ban him from the dramatic play area? Should he even be with these other kids?

I also think of how confused and upset Alex must be. I know he needs kindness and caring, but it's so hard to give it to him when I see this inappropriate behavior. What should I do?

Discussion questions

1. What advice can you give Lynn? What are some ways to get Alex to stop the inappropriate behavior? Think about the pros and cons of each choice.

2. Why do you think Alex spends so much time in the dramatic play area?

3. What do you think Alex needs to support his social/emotional stability?

4. What would you say to the parents in the class who are concerned about the effect of Alex's behavior on their children?

5. What professional resources are available to help Lynn work more effectively with Alex?

How Much Should I Help?

Laurie wonders how much she can help a homeless girl in her first-grade classroom. Should she buy Yolanda things she needs or provide her with new clothes? Will this offend the child's mother? What else can she do to help?

Yolanda skips into my classroom this morning and gives me a big hug. I can feel her bones through her thin cotton dress. I ask her if she had any breakfast.

"No, my brother dropped me off this morning, so we didn't have time to get anything."

Our school has a government-funded breakfast program, but the children have to get to school a half hour before classes start because the cafeteria closes.

I reach into my cabinet and pull out a granola bar for Yolanda. "Eat it quickly, because we're going to get started soon." I keep a small supply of quick snacks for just such occasions.

I teach in a community with a wide variety of children. Many different racial and ethnic groups are represented, but what makes it unusual, I think, is the wide range of socioeconomic differences. We are located in a small city near a large research university, but the economic conditions outside the university community are not good. I therefore have affluent children whose parents hold Ph.D.s sitting next to children from very poor families whose parents may be unemployed or hold minimum wage jobs.

Yolanda's mother has been out of work for a while. Eventually she couldn't afford the rent for their apartment, so she, Yolanda, and Yolanda's brother participate in a program designed to help homeless women with children get back on their feet. In this program the families stay at different churches in the area. During the day they are in one church, then they move to another to sleep. Each week the families rotate to two other churches. They are allowed to stay in the program for only a few months, and during that time the

mothers must be drug- and alcohol-free. The program also has support services to help the mothers find a job and get transportation, an apartment, clothing, and occasionally furniture.

Sometimes Yolanda looks exhausted, and I can understand why. It must be difficult moving from place to place. When I think of some of the children in my class who have beautiful suburban homes with fully furnished bedrooms of their own, toys galore, and big backyards, I want to cry because the world is so unjust. I want Yolanda to have that too.

I desperately want to help Yolanda and give her some of the things she needs. I have already bought her a set of markers, colored pencils, composition books, scissors, and pencils to use at school. Our school expects the parents to contribute these things, but I know Yolanda just won't have them.

When Yolanda had her birthday last week, I bought her one of my favorite children's books and a stuffed animal. I gave them to her after school so the other children wouldn't notice. I felt a little strange doing this, but I was worried that Yolanda wouldn't get any presents. We had a party for her in school, as we do for all the children, and I brought in cupcakes I made myself. After all, how could Yolanda's mother make cupcakes while moving from church to church?

I also give Yolanda time to do her homework in school during center time. I'm not sure if the other children notice this or not. How can I expect her to get anything done otherwise? She has neither a desk nor the materials to work with outside school.

Giving It Some Thought

Yolanda owns only about three outfits. Not only does her mother not have the money to buy more, but it is also difficult to carry lots of belongings from church to church. It's starting to get colder outside, though, and I'm worried about Yolanda having warm clothes and a winter coat. I have two nieces who seem to outgrow things overnight, and I would love to bring some of their things to give Yolanda, but I don't know if it is appropriate.

How much should I help her? Will her mother be offended? What other things can I do?

Discussion questions

1. How much do you think Laurie should help Yolanda in terms of buying her presents or giving her clothes? What is your advice?

2. In what other ways can Laurie help Yolanda besides providing things she needs?

3. Should children who are homeless or very poor get special treatment in school? For example, should they be allowed to do their homework during school time?

4. What are the emotional needs that Yolanda and her mother might have as a result of their living conditions?

5. How can Abraham Maslow's ideas about motivation help us understand this case better?

A Death in Our Class

Mrs. Berman is shocked by the news of the death of one of the children in her preschool class of 4-year-olds. She wonders what to say to the children and how to handle the religious questions that keep coming up.

It was Sunday morning when I got the phone call from Matthew's mother. I can't imagine her agony in calling me, the preschool teacher, to say that her 4-year-old son had died. This kind of thing does not really happen. Not to someone I know. Not to a child in my class. The death was sudden— a terrible accident at a family party on Saturday. No one could have foreseen it.

I had last seen Matthew at school on Friday, which was Halloween. I can close my eyes and still see him in his homemade lion costume, playing with the other children. The day was hectic, as it always is for holiday celebrations, and I was especially upset after the children had been dismissed when I realized that the diamond from my wedding ring had fallen out. After searching everywhere that afternoon, and again on Saturday, I ended up in tears. The ring was very important to me. "How can I replace something with so much sentimental value?" I thought sadly.

Well, after Mrs. Wright's phone call Sunday, all I could think was how incredibly unimportant the diamond really was. How could I have considered it such a big deal?

As I struggled with the shock and my own deep sadness, I realized I had to face the other parents and children at the preschool the next day. Switching to autopilot, I began making calls to start our phone chain. Eventually all the parents in the class were notified and invited to come to the school the next day, if they wanted to, when I planned to speak about Matthew's death at circle time. In a way the telephone calls and plans for Monday helped me, giving me something to focus on.

As I thought more and more about what to say the next day, I realized how difficult and uncomfortable I would be. How could I explain death to 4-year-olds? What could they understand? What could I say that would make them feel better?

Having taught preschool for 20 years, I thought I was well seasoned. After all, I had been through many guinea pig deaths that I had handled with grace and sensitivity. I felt that I had really "done my job" in preparing children for the naturalness and inevitability of death. Now I realized how foolish I was to think that an animal's death could prepare us for what I was feeling at this time!

Of course I kept coming back to the fact that in our preschool—a laboratory school at a large university—religion is not an option for explanations or comfort. Although the class had little racial diversity, we had a good deal of religious diversity. I hoped the parents all would have given their own explanations and shared their beliefs before the children arrived at school. I finally decided that I would focus on feelings. I wrote out what I planned to say so that I would have some security and I wouldn't have to wing it.

The next day, circle time went as well as it could have, I guess, given the upsetting circumstances. I explained that everyone would miss Matthew a great deal and for a while many people would be sad. We talked about different feelings and all the ways we show that we are sad. I tried to let the children know that feeling sad was okay and that the grownups in their lives would be sad too.

I also told the children that Matthew would never come back. I wanted to make sure they all understood the finality of death. I finished up by explaining that everybody's family has different ways of thinking about death and what happens when people die. I told them they should to talk to their families about it.

The children listened carefully, and I made it through my prepared presentation without stumbling or breaking into tears. The parents said subdued goodbyes to their children, and we got on with the day. I have to admit, most of the children eased right back into their routine. A few seemed downcast and quiet, but I thought we'd make it through the morning session without a major breakdown.

Just when I thought I was handling the situation well, controlling my own feelings and supporting the children's, Sandra sat down at the art table next to me.

"Matthew's in heaven, right, Mrs. Berman? My mom says now he's happy with Jesus to take care of him."

I felt my stomach churn. A small group was sitting at the table with us, waiting for my reply. What was I to say? If I said yes, other children who heard me might be confused or tell their parents that I thought Matthew was in heaven with Jesus. Of course I couldn't say no. And if I said I really didn't know, it might upset Sandra's sense of security about what her mom said. Maybe I should have said something different when we discussed this earlier at circle time.

Sandra looked up at me again. What could I say now?

Discussion questions

1. What should Mrs. Berman say to Sandra? What alternatives can you think of to do or say in this situation?

2. From your knowledge of child development, what is a typical 4-year-old's understanding of death? How does knowing this help you plan for the children's needs?

3. What role should religion play in a nonsectarian school such as this one? Is it possible or appropriate to avoid discussing religious ideas, especially when dealing with death? Are there ways to discuss religious ideas while still respecting a diversity of beliefs?

4. What would you have said about Matthew's death at circle time? Describe to your partner or group what points you would have covered.

5. What support do children need to deal with the death of a classmate in a case such as this? What specific actions can Mrs. Berman take to help the children with their feelings?

Stressed-Out Children

Margarita wonders what effect the terrible living conditions and other stressful home situations have on the behavior of the children in her public school kindergarten class. She conducts an experiment in her class to find out and is very surprised by the results.

As I stand in the doorway of my kindergarten classroom, I am overwhelmed thinking about the family lives of many of my children.

Michael has come to school today wearing the same dirty blue jeans and thread-bare T-shirt that he has worn for two weeks. He smells bad and is getting a skin rash.

Tracey's older brother brought her to school today. He explained in his adolescent way that his mother (who has a history of drug and alcohol abuse) couldn't make it out of bed to get Tracey off to school, so he walked her over.

Sandra just said goodbye to her mom. She comes every day, clean as a whistle, with her black hair in perfect braids. She only has a few

outfits, but she is always clean and neat. I learned just last week that she has been living in a shelter with her mom. They had been staying with Sandra's aunt, but she was arrested, so now they need to find another place to live.

Ibn often comes to school looking sad.

His father is in prison, recently convicted of a shooting during a drug deal.

These are only a few of the problems that my children face each day. I teach in a public school in a rough neighborhood of a large city. Most of my students come from low-income housing projects in the surrounding area. For many of them school is a safe haven and the only stability in their lives.

This past semester I took a graduate course in early childhood education at the state college in our city. We were assigned a research project: select a topic, collect information, describe and analyze it, and draw conclusions about what we learned. I thought about the many areas I am interested in and kept coming back to the problems my kids face and the stress in their lives.

What I most wondered about was what effect all this stress has on the children's behavior in school. I have many social problems in my classroom—hitting, fighting, tantrums, and so on. My kids sometimes seem to be filled with anger and frustration, and it comes out in their interactions with each other. They are often right on the edge of losing control—one small incident will upset them to the point of taking physical action.

While reading about the effects of stress on young children, I came across a book by David Elkind in which he describes a scale to measure the amount of stress in a child's life. The scale assigns a number value to life events, both positive and negative, that cause stress. As I looked over the list, it dawned on me that it represents middle-class experiences; the problems that my kids face every day are not even on the list.

I shared this list with Brooke, my assistant teacher, and we decided to develop our own stress scale. We thought about the real-life experiences of our kids and then made a list of them, assigning each experience a numerical value according to how much stress we felt it caused. We were able to "score" the amount of stress in each child's life and rank the children accordingly. Next we created an observation sheet to record the classroom behaviors that we felt were caused by stress. This was based on our opinions and experience, but we knew it would tell us more about our kids.

We took turns observing the children for a few weeks and checked off the stress behaviors that we observed in each. Then we compared children's stress scores with their stress behaviors to find the connection between stress and behavior. I have to admit that we were very surprised by what we found.

Some of the children who scored highest for stress in their lives showed relatively few stress behaviors, while others with lower stress scores showed a lot of stress behaviors. In other words, it seemed to us that some of the children with a great deal of stress in their lives seemed to be affected by the stress while others didn't.

Now we were faced with a different question: What makes some children more resilient than others? What is it that seems to help them cope better?

Discussion questions

1. What do you think Margarita means by *stress behaviors*? What would you look for if you were going to observe stress behaviors?

2. What do you think makes the difference in the more resilient children's lives? How can Erik Erikson's ideas help us understand this problem? How about Abraham Maslow's?

3. What would you as a teacher do to help these children deal with the stress in their lives? What would you do to reduce the stress behaviors in the classroom?

4. How can the information Margarita and Brooke collected help them in working with the families of their children?

5. What follow-up study do you think Margarita and Brooke could conduct that would provide more information about this topic?

Resources for further reading

Blecher-Sass, H. 1997. Goodbyes can build trust. *Young Children* 52 (7): 12–14.
   This article describes how separation can be a positive experience when good relationships are established between caregivers and parents, with ample time allowed for parents to be in the classroom environment. To ease separation anxiety, the author offers 10 practical suggestions for smooth transitions.

Boxhill, N.A. 1994. Making a place for Nona: Meeting the needs of homeless children. *Child Care Information Exchange* (95): 35–37.
   This article discusses the dilemmas that homeless children face and ways that staff can help meet their needs.

Elkind, D. 1981. *The hurried child: Growing up too fast too soon.* Rev. ed. Reading, MA: Addison-Wesley.
   The focus of this book is the overwhelming pressures that American children face, sometimes unwittingly put on them by their parents, schools, and society in general. Elkind examines the many kinds of stress that impact children and how children react to stress. Included is a stress test for children that charts the impact of the various changes in a child's life that hurry and stress them.

Erikson, E.H. 1963. *Childhood and society.* New York: Norton.
   This landmark work on the social significance of childhood has greatly influenced modern understanding of human development. Outlining eight stages in emotional development, this book also explains a psychoanalytic perspective of early childhood. Included are case studies and anecdotes to illustrate the main ideas.

Essa, E. 1995. Death of a friend. *Childhood Education* 71 (3): 130–33.
   This article tells the story of a young boy's death and describes the communication, reactions, and experiences that were helpful in his coping with this event.

Good, L.A. 1996. When a child has been sexually abused: Several resources for parents and early childhood professionals. *Young Children* 51 (5): 84–85.
   This succinct article provides information on how early childhood educators can help children deal with the trauma of sexual abuse. It also provides a resource list and children's book recommendations.

Gunsberg, A. 1989. Empowering young abused and neglected children through contingency play. *Childhood Education* 66 (1): 8–10.
   Through a case study of a 4-year-old girl, this article describes the helpful intervention of contingency play to reduce stress and develop positive coping behaviors.

Maslow, A.H. 1999. *Toward a psychology of being.* 3d ed. New York: Wiley.
   This book outlining Maslow's theories of self-actualization and hierarchy of needs has become a classic in educational psychology. Maslow identifies in an optimistic way the intrinsic values present in childhood and humanity, while offering insight into learners' motivations.

Mazur, S., & C. Pekor. 1985. Viewpoint. Can teachers touch children anymore? Physical contact and its value in child development. *Young Children* 40 (4): 10–12.

The challenges of balancing the physical nurturance of children with the public's concern about the sexual abuse of young children are the main focus of this article. Also examined are the public's perception of child care, parent and professional concerns, and the implications for child development.

McCracken, J.B., ed. 1986. *Reducing stress in young children's lives*. Washington, DC: NAEYC.

This compilation of articles published in *Young Children* is grouped by topics such as coping with unexpected challenges, strengthening contemporary families, ensuring that adults don't contribute to children's stress, and a review of the research on stress in young children.

Miller, K. 1996. *The crisis manual for early childhood teachers: How to handle the really difficult problems.* Beltsville, MD: Gryphon House.

This is a thorough source book to help teachers deal with crises in children's lives. Advice on the caregiver's role and general problem-solving strategies are given along with chapters on specific situations such as death, homelessness, child abuse and sexual abuse, family illness, and divorce.

NAEYC. 1997. NAEYC position statement on the prevention of child abuse in early childhood programs and the responsibilities of early childhood professionals to prevent child abuse. *Young Children* 52 (3): 42–46.

This position statement outlines recommendations on early childhood program policies, staff screening, recruitment, retention, and policies to promote partnerships with families.

Slavenas, R. 1988. The role and responsibility of teachers and child care workers in identifying and reporting child abuse and neglect. *Early Child Development and Care* 31: 19–25.

This article gives a clear, brief overview of the responsibilities of early childhood professionals in preventing, identifying, and reporting child abuse and neglect.

Werner, E.E. 1984. Research in review. Resilient children. *Young Children* 40 (1): 68–72.

This articles identifies central characteristics that are common in resilient children and the factors within and outside the family that contribute to resiliency. It also discusses the implications for early childhood educators.

6

Challenges in
Antibias Practice

"Boys Will Be Boys"

Sharise and Patty debate what they could have done when their 3- and 4-year-olds all picked gender stereotyped roles to play during a simulation of beehive activity.

Patty and I are coteachers of our twenty-two 3- to 5-year-olds. We work in a campus laboratory school, which enables us to have a program that we feel is exemplary. We are fortunate to have a large, well-equipped classroom and college students to assist us with the children. Many of the children's parents work for the college, but we also have a good percentage of children from working-class families who have heard by word-of-mouth how good our program is.

Patty and I have worked together for two years, and we get along very well. We don't always see eye to eye, but we share similar philosophies. We have tried different approaches to planning our curriculum together and taking responsibility for the class. We usually decide together on the general framework for our activities. One of us then takes responsibility for planning the details of an activity, gathering materials, and leading the activity. We take turns throughout the week, and it seems to work smoothly.

This week we began activities centered around the theme of bees. Patty took charge of our circle time today, which gave me a chance to watch the children more closely. This is one of the great benefits of coteaching—we can really step back and observe, thereby getting to know the children better.

After reading them a short informational book about bees and how they work together with different "jobs," Patty had the children pretend to be different kinds of bees. Offering props she had gathered, Patty gave the children the choice of being the cleaner bees that keep the hive neat, the protector bees that keep strangers from entering the hive, the queen bee and those bees that help with the newborn bees, the worker bees that go out to get the nectar to make into honey, and the bees that make new cells for the hive. The children had a wonderful time creating their own beehive of activity.

At the end of the day, as we were cleaning up, I complimented Patty on her creative ideas. "Thanks, Sharise," she said. "How do you think the beehive activity went?"

"The children really enjoyed it. I got the sense that they understood how all the bees had their own jobs but were still part of the whole hive. I think the message of teamwork got through to them," I replied.

"What did you think about who chose which roles?" Patty asked.

"Well, I noticed that the girls chose to be the helpers to the queen and the cleaner bees. The boys rushed to guard the hive and build new honeycomb cells. The bees gathering nectar were an equal mix of boys and girls. Since you hadn't talked about gender differences in the bees except for the queen, the gender role stereotyping surprised me!" I exclaimed.

"I agree. When I watched the girls running around sweeping and vacuuming and the boys threatening strangers with imaginary swords, I was surprised at how much the gender-based choices bothered me. We work so hard to counter those gender influences, yet sometimes I feel we haven't made much of a difference at all!"

Giving It Some Thought

"I know what you mean, Patty. Even though the boys wander over to cook dinner in the play kitchen and the girls build in the block area, we still have a long way to go."

"I thought about raising the issue of what roles the boys picked and what roles the girls picked, but I didn't know whether it was a good idea to bring it to the children's attention," Patty added.

"I don't know either. Let's think about it and bring it up at our next staff meeting. I'm curious to hear what ideas the other teachers have about handling the kids' choices!"

Discussion questions

1. If you were at the staff meeting, what advice would you give Patty and Sharise about handling the choices of role-playing in the beehive activity?

2. Do you think that gender stereotypes are a problem? Why or why not?

3. What specific suggestions would you offer to preschool teachers who want to discourage gender stereotyping in their classrooms?

4. In what ways do teachers often unconsciously contribute to gender stereotyping?

5. How do gender roles develop in young children? What role does culture play in determining gender roles?

What's So Bad about Parties?

In her preschool class for children with special needs, Dawn has a boy who is a Jehovah's Witness. She has a difficult time honoring his parents' request that he not participate in school parties. Dawn thinks Darryl's parents don't understand how left out he feels, so one day she lets him participate in a class birthday celebration.

I still feel bad when I think back on one of my worst days of teaching.

I was the teacher of a preschool class for children with special needs in a large urban public school in an economically depressed city. I had a class of eight children with only two girls. Some of the children were Hispanic, one was of Irish descent, one Haitian, and one child Darryl was African American and Hispanic.

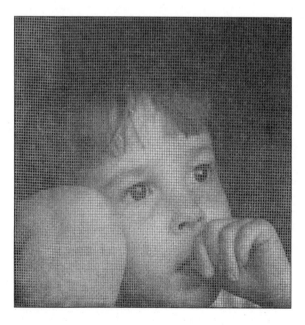

Darryl was classified as having a communication disability, but he was very bright and his parents had high expectations for him. They themselves were high achievers and placed a lot of demands on Darryl.

One day early in the year, after we had completed a holiday art project, Darryl's parents sent me a note explaining that they were Jehovah's Witnesses, so Darryl

Giving It Some Thought

couldn't participate in certain activities. They came in the next day and gave me a booklet that explained the beliefs and practices of Jehovah's Witnesses. This information was very helpful, and I promised I would do my best to follow their request.

A few weeks later Darryl's parents came in again and gave me a booklet explaining how teachers should teach their child. This time I got the uncomfortable feeling that they wanted me to endorse their values. I could respect their religious beliefs and I could do my best to keep Darryl from participating in inappropriate activities, but I was offended at what I interpreted as their attempts to convert me.

I guess I really was intolerant, but I felt that what his parents were asking me to do unfairly restricted Darryl from taking part in group activities with the other kids. When parents send their children to public school, don't they have to expect to compromise?

This was my eleventh year of teaching and I used cultural and religious holidays to organize the curriculum. I celebrated everything—Chinese New Year, St. Patrick's Day, Los Posados, Groundhog Day, Passover, Easter, and so on. I wanted my children to be exposed to many cultures and beliefs. But Darryl was not allowed to participate in any celebrations or art activities connected to holidays.

Especially difficult were birthday parties. Parents would send in Barbie-theme paper plates and hats, fancy cakes, and goodie bags. I would take Darryl to another teacher's class while we had the party. Even at 4 years he must have known he was missing something. I think he felt it was punishment.

I tried not to use the word *party,* but of course the children did. Whenever there were goodie bags, I would place Darryl's in his cubby and tell him it was for doing good work that day. I thought if I called it a party bag, his parents wouldn't let him have it.

In December the Rotary Club brought Christmas presents to the school and a dressed-up Santa visited us. I had to send Darryl to another room, but I unwrapped his gift and gave it to him later, saying it was a reward for good academic work.

One day when we were planning to celebrate a birthday, as it got close to snack time, I walked Darryl down the hall with his snack. "Mrs. M says you can come and eat snack in her room today," I said in a cheerful voice. But Darryl started to cry and said he wanted to stay in our room.

At this point I felt great anger toward Darryl's parents. I felt that they were making him suffer and they didn't realize the consequences. It broke my heart. He was so young, how could he understand? I just didn't know how to communicate to him why he couldn't participate in some activities but not others. And his difficulty with communication increased his frustration. Darryl was so upset I decided to let him stay for the party. How would his parents ever know?

For this birthday party the children had Star Wars hats, plates, and napkins, and the cake was shaped like a large number 5. We sang an enthusiastic round of "Happy Birthday" and Martin blew out the candles. As I put the knife into the cake, I looked up and saw Darryl's mother standing in the doorway. I wanted to sink under the table.

What was I going to say now?

Discussion questions

1. Retell this case from the point of view of Darryl's mother. What do you think she feels? What should Dawn say now?

2. Dawn says that when you send your child to a public school, you need to compromise. Do you agree? Why or why not?

3. What role should holidays play in early childhood curriculum? How can holidays be celebrated in culturally sensitive ways?

4. Should you gather information about the cultural and religious traditions of your students? Why or why not? If you decided to gather such information, how would you do it?

5. Should religion be part of the early childhood curriculum? If not, why not? If yes, how should it be included?

Speaking Our Language

Veronica is faced with a tough decision when she begins her new job as a teaching assistant in a class of 3- and 4-year-olds in an international preschool. She feels that the lead teacher is using inappropriate practices in forcing the children to speak only English.

When I began my new job working at an international preschool, I was excited because the school had been highly recommended by many people. I was hired as a part-time floater in the mornings and an assistant teacher in the afternoons. I considered this to be an ideal situation—to have exposure to different age groups and different teaching styles. My first floating position was in a classroom of older 3-year-old and young 4-year-old children.

My first day began at 8:20 A.M. with the children saying goodbye to their parents or caregivers. As the children entered the classroom, they immediately sat at a table to do written work on a photocopied sheet with the letter *E* drawn like an elephant. When the worksheet was completed, they moved to the arts and crafts table.

The teacher Adrienne told the children, "Be quiet and pay attention to your work." A few children were talking and fooling around with some of the materials. Adrienne admonished them for not doing their work and told them they were being naughty and lazy. She praised the ones who did their work, usually saying "Good girl!" (I noticed that in most cases girls followed her instructions and boys were yelled at.)

Two Japanese children spoke in their native language as they completed their work. Adrienne reprimanded them repeatedly with, "You are in America now, speak English!" These two little boys immediately stopped talking and went back to work. I did not see them talking to each other again that morning.

Next the children went to the gym. During this activity time they played organized games such as Duck, Duck, Goose and Have You Ever Seen a Lassie? This lasted for fifteen minutes, and then the children were allowed free play for the remaining time in gym. Two of the older girls began to play a rhythmic clapping game in their home language, which I thought was perhaps German. Adrienne came over and gently but firmly told them to stop. She joined the girls' circle and started them chanting Miss Mary Mack.

When we returned to the classroom, I assumed the children would have some time for dramatic play, blocks, art, and sensory activities at the well-equipped centers around the room. However, the children were immediately instructed to sit down on the rug for circle time.

During circle time Adrienne took attendance and proceeded to ask Rachel what day it was. Rachel spoke only a few words of English, so she tried to answer but soon gave up. Adrienne, however, insisted on a response. When she started asking other questions about the calendar, some of the other children looked uncomfortable and held their heads down so Adrienne couldn't see their faces.

When circle time ended, the children moved over to the tables for more teacher-directed activities. Adrienne carefully separated the two girls who had played the clapping game and seated the two Japanese boys at different tables. She also reminded a few of the other children that only English was allowed at school. The children had little time to play or interact socially, which I felt would help their English ability.

I wrote down some of my observations about this classroom. The next day I discussed my experiences with my director Mrs. Taylor. I told her that I was surprised at what I had seen in this classroom. I thought the children's home cultures were being denied and that it was not right that the children were never allowed to speak anything but English. The whole time I was in the room, there had been no acknowledgment of other cultures or languages.

Mrs. Taylor nodded in understanding and said, "Adrienne has been teaching for 35 years. Some parents prefer her traditional style of teaching. They want their children assimilated quickly into American culture because they think it will help prepare them for school. Many of the parents ask us to have their children speak only English while they are here."

I replied in frustration, "This is not helping the children prepare for school because it hurts their sense of who they are. And they are being denied the opportunity to learn concepts because they don't always understand English." I added, "Isn't it our job as educators to do what we really believe is right for children and help parents understand that?"

I could see I wasn't going to change Mrs. Taylor's mind very easily. I realized that I had an important decision to make. Should I remain in this classroom and try subtly and gradually to help Adrienne understand how important it is to accept and validate the children's cultures? Should I ask the director to assign me to another classroom? Or should I just find another job at a school that better matches my philosophy?

Discussion questions

1. What choice would you make if you were in Veronica's position? Why?

2. Do you agree with the director's assessment that Adrienne's teaching is acceptable because many parents want their children to learn English quickly? Why or why not?

3. Do you think this description of Adrienne's classroom represents practices that are not appropriate for young children? What specifically do you think might be inappropriate? Why? How can Lev Vygotsky and Mikhail Bakhtin's ideas about sociocultural learning help us analyze this case?

4. What role should parents have in deciding the type of classroom practices that take place in their child's classroom? How do Reggio Emilia schools compare to this one?

5. By retelling or through role play, consider this case from the perspectives of both Adrienne and one of the parents at the school. What have you learned from examining their viewpoints?

Will He Be Gay if He Plays with Dolls?

Rita has a kindergarten boy who prefers to play with girls and dolls. His mother is worried that this behavior will influence his sexual preference later in life and asks Rita to try to get him to identify more with the boys.

Garret is probably one of the smartest kids in my class. He is a joy to have around—always asking interesting questions and examining things with an intense curiosity. He is also kind and gentle and well liked by my class of 20 White, middle-class kindergartners.

Most of the children come from two-parent families in which the mother is at home full-time or part-time to take care of the children. Garret is no exception. His mom Sylvia, a journalist, has suspended her career to be home with Garret and his younger sister.

Garret's father is a high-profile lawyer, and although he seemed very caring when I saw him with his kids, Garret's mother told me he works long hours, usually coming home after the kids are in bed and leaving early in the morning, and he goes away frequently on long business trips.

When I had my first parent conference with Garret's mom in October, I told her how well Garret was doing academically. He could already read simple chapter books and was way ahead of the class in his math reasoning. She seemed pleased with my comments but immediately asked me with whom he played and what kinds of things he liked to do.

"Well, Garret has already made a few good friends. He plays with Alicia, Veronica, and Patty just about every day. They love the dress-up clothes and usually play in the housekeeping corner. They also like to write stories and illustrate them," I told her.

"Does he ever play with the boys?" asked Sylvia.

"Oh sure, whenever we work in groups he gets along well with all the other kids," I explained.

"But during center time does he ever choose to work with boys?" she prodded.

"Gee, I'm not sure. I don't really remember him joining in with their play. He usually works by himself or with a few of the girls. Why do you ask?"

"We are worried about Garret. Ever since he was in preschool, he has said that he wants to be a girl. He loves girl things. He plays only with girls. He would wear girls clothes if we let him, but we don't. We just started taking him to a psychologist who thinks Garret has some difficulty with his gender identity. To be honest, we're afraid if we don't intervene, Garret will end up being gay," Sylvia said.

She went on to ask for my help in getting him to associate more with boys and build up his sense of male identity. I promised her I would do what I could.

Now that Sylvia has made me aware of it, I can see why she is so concerned. Garret never spontaneously joins the boys in their play. He prefers quieter activities like art, and he loves to play with dolls in the housekeeping corner. Given the choice, he always picks a pink cupcake or the pink paper to draw on. He loves playing with the girls' hair and admires their dresses.

Of course Garret's only 5 years old, I keep telling myself. Are his parents making a mountain out of a molehill? I wonder if he prefers girls and "girl things" because he spends so much time with his mother and doesn't have his father around much as a role model. I think I see a lot of his behaviors in other kids too, maybe just not as much as in Garret.

What I really worry about is how the other

kids are beginning to treat Garret. Occasionally some of the boys tease him about being a "girl." They joke about him wearing the feminine dress-up clothes. Yesterday I heard one of the boys call him a "queer" out on the playground. How does a kindergartner even know what *queer* means?

I really don't know how much I can do to help Garret. I think there's always the chance that other children will be cruel, especially as he gets older, but maybe we should respect his choices. I have always hated all the gender stereotypes and how they restrict girls. Now I realize those stereotypes are just as damaging to boys.

Will Garret be gay because he plays with dolls? What if a person really is born gay? Are we hurting or helping Garret by trying to push behavior that may not be natural for him?

Discussion questions

1. What do you know about gender role development in early childhood that can help shed light on this case? What information about how sexual preferences develop would help Garret's teacher and family make decisions?

2. Rita says that she has seen many of Garret's behaviors in other children but not to the same degree. What behaviors have you seen in young children that go against typical gender stereotypes?

3. What role does culture play in this case? How many cultural differences in accepted gender-based behaviors can you identify?

4. Do you think it is the role of the teacher to discourage children from demonstrating behaviors that go against gender stereotypes? For example, should teachers discourage or encourage boys playing with dolls? How would your answer change based on the age of the child in question?

5. What advice can you give to a teacher like Rita, who prefers to break gender stereotypes, in a situation in which a child's parent asks her specifically to reinforce them?

I Am Child—Hear Me Roar!

Nancy, a veteran teacher, questions the lack of balance between building children's self-esteem and preparing them for the harsh realities of the world in which they are growing up. Are we allowing children to become too comfortable? Too self-involved? How will children learn to compete when they have been coddled into believing they should always feel good?

I've heard much roaring during the past few years of my nearly three decades of teaching young children. It started with a childrearing philosophy that advised parents to deeply instill their child with self-confidence. This, says the theory, helps a child be less fearful of taking risks and therefore more willing to investigate and learn. Such children will be prepared to face any odds because they "feel good about themselves."

I believe this theory looks great on paper but in practice has backfired. I wonder whether I can—or should—do anything about it.

This year I have a multiage group of 4- to 6-year-olds in the child care center where I teach. The children in my class are so self-confident and feel so good about themselves that they expect me to do everything for them. When their shoelaces come untied, they think I should tie them. When they bang their cups on the table, they expect me to pour their milk. They push other children away to claim their "rightful place" at the head of the line. They are so full of themselves that they defy their parents and their teachers.

Some experts may say these children have leadership potential. But I wonder, What is wrong with being a follower?

Well-meaning, loving parents allow their children to win at board games, hesitate to use the *N* word (*No!*), and praise a lot and reprimand little, all in the name of building their children's self-confidence. These children have come to believe they are always right.

Last week Min, one of the 5-year-old boys in my class, began to shake another child's chair at the snack table. I asked him to stop, but he then stood behind the chair and rocked it back and forth until Thomas started to fall off. To prevent Thomas from getting hurt, I sent Min to time-out in the book corner until snack was over. While he was there I explained to him that I can't let anyone hurt another child.

The next day Min's father told me that he did not want Min sent to time-out again. He felt it was humiliating to his son and that I should reprimand him privately. He did not want Min's self-esteem damaged.

I felt frustrated. How could I possibly have a safe and orderly classroom if I couldn't allow children to feel bad about what they'd done wrong? Don't children have to develop a conscience? How else will they learn to behave in society?

Our schools and child care centers seem to foster the philosophy that self-esteem is more important than anything else. I have taught for 26 years in our center, I have raised my own children, and I have seen the subtle changes over the years. For example, competition is now frowned upon; everyone must win at all the games. Stickers are given for almost any level of effort. We are cautioned against using negative directions containing the words *no, don't,* or *wrong.* "Don't climb that fence" becomes "Our school is a safe place. We

Giving It Some Thought

keep our feet on the ground." Our favorite songs include "I Am Special" and "I Like Me."

Yes, young children need self-confidence and support to learn—no argument there. But have adults gone overboard? The issue poses some ethical and moral questions for me.

What ever happened to humility? Don't rewards and success need to be earned to be meaningful? How will these me-oriented children fare in public school when faced with competition? Am I an old fuddy-duddy who still wants to live in Mr. Rogers' Neighborhood?

Discussion questions

1. How important do you feel self-esteem is in helping children succeed? What do you know about child development that helps you decide?

2. How can Erik Erikson's theory of psychosocial development help in understanding the psychological needs of young children? How does this affect the analysis of the case? Would your answer change if these children were 10 years old? Two years old?

3. Is self-esteem the only issue in this case? Are there other aspects of Nancy's dilemma that you can identify? Brainstorm as many as possible.

4. How important is competition in our society? What do you think the role of competition should be in our schools? Please support your answer.

5. What can and should teachers do when they find philosophical differences between the practices expected at their school or center and their own personal beliefs?

"White Girl"

Carmen is shocked during her first-grade teaching practicum experience when one of the children calls her "White girl" and complains about Carmen not paying attention to her. She wonders what to do or say.

I have been assigned to observe and help out in Mrs. Berilla's first-grade class each Wednesday this semester in conjunction with a course in educational psychology that is part of the university's teacher training program. This is my fourth visit, and overall everything was running smoothly until today. The school is in a large city and all of the children are Black—either African, African American, or Caribbean. Some are biracial. Being Portuguese and having learned English as a second language, I felt that I knew very personally what it was like to be a minority member.

The children seemed happy to see me today. As they walked into the classroom, they looked for me at the small table in the back of the room, where I usually sit, and waved. Those sitting close to my table walked over and whispered good morning to me. Tanisha, who sits closest to me, had latched on to me right away. I was flattered by the attention from her and the other children.

From my first day in class, my cooperating teacher has allowed me to do reading time with the children. Today I read a book by Paul Rogers, *What Will the Weather Be Like Today?* and held a discussion about weather. Then the students went to their desks to write and draw pictures about the weather on the colorful construction paper I had brought.

I walked around the room giving them feedback on what a great job they were doing. That's when I noticed Tanisha following me. When I asked her to sit down and wait till I got to her table, she said, "I'm done."

I looked at Tanisha's blank paper and told her once more to sit down and do her work. "When I get to your desk, I will look at what you've done, Tanisha," I said.

Tanisha went back to her seat, but when I got to her desk she was standing up next to her chair. I looked at her paper and asked her why she hadn't drawn or written anything. "Because I want you to do it with me," Tanisha replied.

At that moment Courtney, sitting next to her, handed me her paper. I looked at it and praised her work.

All of a sudden I heard "Hey!" It was Tanisha. I looked in her direction and she whispered to me, "You White girl think you can come into my classroom and pay attention to me on some days but not on others?"

I was unable to reply. I just stood there staring. Maybe I misunderstood her, I thought. But no, Tanisha started repeating the sentence over and over, apparently realizing the effect it had on me.

I thought young children didn't notice race, let alone have such strong feelings about it. Here I was paralyzed in front of a first-grade child, not able to respond to her powerful words. And Tanisha was still waiting for a response.

Discussion questions

1. What response do you think Carmen should give to Tanisha? Why?

2. What do you know about how young children learn about racial differences and develop their own sense of identity? Should Carmen be surprised at this challenge from a first-grader? How would Carmen's response to this change if Tanisha were 4 years old? Twelve years old?

3. Why do you think Tanisha felt that race affected the way Carmen treated her?

4. What can teachers of young children do to combat racism and build racial understanding and acceptance? List as many specific ideas as you can.

5. What examples of institutional racism can you identify? For example, in the school in which Carmen teaches, the students are all children of color while the teachers and principals are White. What message does this send about power relations? Try to identify other instances of this kind of racism. What effect does this have on young children?

"You Can't Play with Us"

Carol is faced with a growing problem in her second-grade class. The children are isolating a Native American girl who has recently moved into their small rural town. Carol wonders how she can include antibias activities in her curriculum and what role parents can play in combating this occurrence of racism.

"Can I play with you?" asks Lieta as she approaches the girls in the game center.

"No, we've already started. Sorry," Crystal says and turns back to the other girls, who lean together and giggle.

Since the school year began, I've noticed the subtle ways that Lieta has been isolated in our second-grade classroom. Lieta is a Native American girl with long, straight black hair and dark skin. The rest of the class by contrast is Caucasian, with light skin, blonde or light brown hair, and blue eyes. Unfortunately the children in our small town have not had much firsthand experience with children who look different from themselves.

Lieta moved into town at the end of last year and spent a few months of first grade in our school. The school has only one teacher per grade, so the children stay together in the same group for many years. Lieta's teacher from last year told me that Lieta is shy and did not make many friends. But after all, she had just moved and was new to the group, so the teacher thought things would improve as everyone got to know her.

Well, it doesn't seem to me that things have gotten better at all. I spent the beginning of the school year as I usually do, playing getting-to-know-you games and trying to build community spirit in the class. My goal is to have our class be like a family. The children do many projects in small groups, and I try to rotate the groups' members so that the children get to know each other well.

At this age all the children, and the girls especially, begin to have close friendships and tend to socialize with the same group. I try hard to ensure that no one is left out. This year, however, I'm not having much success. It's November and I think the children are excluding Lieta more now than before.

Unlike her teacher last year, I feel that Lieta is quite sociable and not at all shy. She seems very kind and is keenly interested in what the other children are doing. I often wonder, in fact, if she isn't too forward in her requests to socialize. Somehow it seems that the other children get the wrong signals from her, or maybe she has difficulty understanding their social cues. Either way, during choice time and at lunch and recess, I notice that Lieta frequently gets left out.

I've been trying to convince myself otherwise, but I think the children are reacting to the racial differences between Lieta and themselves. I'm not sure if it's just a matter of her looking different or whether deeper racism is at work here. I wonder what the children's parents might have said about Lieta or her family when they moved into town.

This week parent conferences begin, and I am trying to think of a way to talk to all the parents in the class about this problem without referring to Lieta or mentioning the facts. I'm at a loss for how to do it, though. I have a conference with Lieta's parents tomorrow, and I'm carefully rehearsing what to say to them. Should I mention their daughter's growing isolation? Should I ask her parents for help or advice, or will that just make the situation worse for Lieta?

In my teaching practices I know I need to take a more active stand against racism. I'd like to focus on antibias activities throughout the day, and I'm trying to come up with some good ideas for tying respect for racial and cultural differences into our social studies curriculum as well. But I wonder how much I can expect second-graders to understand.

Discussion questions

1. What suggestions can you give Carol for antibias activities in her second-grade class? What influence does the history of the treatment of Native Americans have on this case?

2. How much about racism can second-graders be expected to understand? Based on your knowledge of the development of social skills, self-concept, and perspective taking in young children, determine what is reasonable to expect.

3. Do you think Carol should discuss this issue with the parents in her class? Why or why not? If she were to bring it up, what might she say?

4. Is it possible to have antibias curriculum in a class that is culturally and racially homogeneous?

5. How do you balance children's need to choose with whom they work and socialize and the needs of the rejected children? Would your answer change based on the age of the children? For example, should kindergartners be able to say they don't want to play with certain children?

Resources for further reading

Almeida, D.A. 1996. *Countering prejudice against American Indians and Alaska Natives through anti-bias curriculum and instruction.* ERIC Digest, ED 400 146.
This ERIC Digest document identifies inadequacies in our current teaching about Native Americans and our conventional multicultural education. It offers suggestions for combating racist portrayals of Native Americans in the larger society and developing antibias curriculum.

Bisson, J. 1997. *Celebrate: An anti-bias guide to enjoying the holidays in early childhood programs.* St. Paul, MN: Redleaf.
This practical guide for teachers struggling with how to enjoy holidays in a respectful, antibias way includes strategies for developing a holiday policy, selecting holidays, addressing stereotypes and commercialism, and evaluating holiday activities. It also includes an extensive list of resources.

Buzelli, C.A. 1995. The development of moral reflection in the early childhood classroom. *Contemporary Education* 66 (3): 143–45.
This article examines the sociocultural approach to moral reflection based on Vygotsky's and Bakhtin's work. This approach provides the rationale for engaging children in authentic, critical communication to develop self-regulation and moral reflection.

Delpit, L. 1995. *Other people's children: Cultural conflict in the classroom.* New York: New Press.
This book presents an honest and piercing discussion of the power imbalances and cultural miscommunication in our schools that lead to the academic problems attributed to children of color.

Derman-Sparks, L., & the A.B.C. Task Force. 1989. *Anti-bias curriculum: Tools for empowering young children.* Washington, DC: NAEYC.

This popular book lays the foundation for early childhood professionals in treating children, families, and each other with respect by confronting, transcending, and eliminating bias related to race, culture, gender, or ability. Chapters cover many topics in antibias curriculum such as learning about racial differences and similarities and learning to resist stereotyping and discriminatory behavior.

Erikson, E.H. 1963. *Childhood and society.* New York: Norton.

This landmark work on the social significance of childhood has greatly influenced modern understanding of human development. Outlining eight stages in emotional development, this book also explains a psychoanalytic perspective of early childhood. Included are case studies and anecdotes to illustrate the main ideas.

Green, E.J. 1997. Guidelines for serving linguistically and culturally diverse young children. *Early Childhood Education Journal* 24 (3): 147–54.

This article discusses demographic trends, second-language acquisition research, bilingual and ESL (English as a Second Language) programs, assessment, controversies, and program recommendations.

Horgan, D.D. 1995. *Achieving gender equity: Strategies for the classroom.* Boston: Allyn & Bacon.

This text gives a clear view of gender inequities illustrated through examples of children's lives in school. Most of the book focuses on specific strategies for teachers to use to achieve gender equity. These include many activities and reproducible forms that can be used in staff meetings, in college classrooms, or individually for reflection and growth.

Jones, E., & L. Derman-Sparks. 1992. Meeting the challenge of diversity. *Young Children* 47 (2): 12–18.

In a clear and direct way, the authors identify inappropriate approaches to diversity in early childhood programs, such as teachers believing they are not prejudiced or being proud to be "colorblind." They suggest practical ways to make changes and provide a checklist to assess an antibias environment.

Mallory, B.L., & R.S. New., eds. 1994. *Diversity and developmentally appropriate practices: Challenges for early childhood education.* New York: Teachers College Press.

This edited volume compiles chapters by various authors who take the position that the way developmentally appropriate practice is currently conceptualized is too narrow. The authors suggest specific ways in which we need to broaden the definition of appropriateness to address cultural and developmental diversity.

NAEYC. 1995. NAEYC Position Statement. Responding to linguistic and cultural diversity—Recommendations for effective early childhood education. *Young Children* 51 (2): 4–12.

This position statement lays out the challenges of responding to linguistic and cultural diversity and provides recommendations for working with children and families, professional preparation, programs, and practice.

Paley., V. 1979. *White teacher.* Cambridge, MA: Harvard University Press.
This classic account of Paley's struggles and reflections on being a White teacher in an integrated class raises many issues of race that are still pertinent today. This book helps teachers look at their own behavior in dealing more openly and constructively with racial differences.

Schaub, M. 1995. *Cross-cultural dialogics: Bakhtinian theory and second language audience.* Paper presented at the Annual Meeting of Conference of Composition and Communication, March, Washington, D.C. ERIC Accession No. ED385163.
The paper outlines the possible impact of Bakhtinian theory concept in ESL (English as a Second Language) instruction. Bakhtin's views on the culturally and politically embedded nature of language are ideal for discussions of cross-cultural communication and apply broadly to all ages, especially early childhood second-language learners.

Teaching Tolerance Project. 1997. *Starting small: Teaching tolerance in preschool and the early grades.* Montgomery, AL: Southern Poverty Law Center.
This book profiles seven classrooms in which teachers are helping children build inclusive, equitable, caring communities. Besides the detailed descriptions of the programs, the book includes reflections linking research and practice and applications offering practical ideas for incorporating concepts into classrooms.

Titone, C., & K.E. Maloney. 1999. *Women's philosophies of education: Thinking through our mothers.* Upper Saddle River, NJ: Merrill.
This text presents the educational thinking of seven women from a variety of times, cultures, and classes whose ideas influence our present educational views. These perspectives add richness to the ways of looking at today's educational challenges.

Vygotsky, L. 1978. *Mind in society: The development of higher psychological processes.* Cambridge, MA: Harvard University Press.
This classic work provides a scholarly foundation of Vygotsky's psychology of learning, including the ideas of the zone of proximal development, language as a social process, the role of egocentric speech, and the relationship between intrapsychological and interpsychological development.

York, S. 1991. *Roots and wings: Affirming culture in early childhood settings.* St. Paul, MN: Redleaf.
This teacher's guide reviews what multicultural education is and why it is important. Practical suggestions for implementing multicultural education are included. A companion volume, *Developing Roots and Wings: A Trainer's Guide to Affirming Culture in Early Childhood Programs,* is available (from the same publisher) for adult educators working with teachers to develop culturally responsive programs.

7

Challenges of Workplace Settings

Why Would a Man Want to Work with Young Children?

Mark loves his job as an assistant teacher in the infant/toddler room, but he is frustrated with people questioning his motives for working with young children and parents' lack of trust in him.

I had just finished changing Margaret's diaper. A small group gathered around me as I sat in the book corner and began reading the pages of *Goodnight Moon*. Joey pushed up as close as he could, and Shelby plopped down in my lap. As we got involved in turning pages, I noticed the director Susan slip into the room, talking quietly with a young couple. The mother was holding a chubby, curly haired, olive-skinned little girl. They all smiled enthusiastically as they watched the children engrossed in the exciting materials in our brightly colored, warm, friendly room.

Then, as their gazes fell in my direction, I saw the familiar response I've come to dread. There was a surprised, questioning look in the parents' eyes, and I noticed both of them whispering to Susan. They watched for a few more minutes before slipping out again. I wondered if they would decide to entrust their daughter to us.

I am a Black male, very tall with long dreadlocks—not your typical child care provider. I love my job but I am frustrated by the way people question my motives in working with young children. I have been an assistant teacher in our infant/toddler room for seven years, and although the staff are very supportive, others outside the center are not.

Our child care center is racially diverse, with many Asian children, some Hispanic, and a few African American and European American. We are on the outskirts of a small city, and most of the parents are professionals.

I began working here after a few other disappointing jobs left me wondering what direction my life should take. I had taken some community college courses, but they weren't for me. Now I am very proud to have earned my Child Development Associate credential from the Council for Early Childhood Professional Recognition. It took me four years of workshops and training sessions, and I feel I earned every bit of this recognition.

Unfortunately, most people just see me as a man working with babies. They are afraid I'm perverted or will molest their young child. I understand their worries in this age of constant media reporting about child abuse cases, but I wish I could change their attitude. I interviewed at five other centers before Susan hired me. I give her a lot of credit for taking a chance and giving me an opportunity to prove myself. I sometimes worry that enrollment will suffer because of my presence in the infant/toddler room.

The parents at the center trust me now, but many of them seemed quite cold at first, until they got to know me. I think it's especially difficult being in the infant/toddler room because the children can't yet tell their parents what we did together during the day or how they feel about me. These young children also need more touching in their daily care, which makes parents nervous. I try to do my share of the diapering and feeding, but I am always aware that when I touch a child or cuddle with a baby, people see my actions with different eyes because I am a man.

When I'm socializing on the weekends or after a long day at work, the last thing I need is people teasing me about my job. Not only

do they have the idea that I am "just babysitting," but they wonder why I'm not doing something more gender appropriate. Most of my friends still think I'm just working here until something better comes along.

Last week a friend called me about a paraprofessional job in the local public school near my house. At first I dismissed the whole idea, but today as the couple left our center to decide whether they could trust me with their little girl, I began to wonder if I should reconsider.

Discussion questions

1. Have you ever encountered the attitude about men working with young children that Mark describes? How do you feel about men working with young children? What do you think are the historical, social, and economic reasons that so few men are found in early childhood settings?

2. What specific actions could the center director take to make parents more comfortable with Mark (or any caregiver) in the infant/toddler room?

3. What kinds of touching are appropriate when working with young children? Discuss this question for children of different ages. What is appropriate for infants? Preschoolers? Second-graders?

4. How would you respond to someone who states that working in a child care center is babysitting?

5. What advice can you give Mark about his job choices? Do you think he'd be better off working with older children? Should he stay in the infant/toddler room? Why or why not?

Working Together:
A Rough Road

Shek-yee encounters difficulty in her class of 4-year-olds at a large Head Start center. Her assistant teacher doesn't agree with her new teaching ideas and wants things done as they had been before Shek-yee took over the class.

On my first day as a head teacher at the city's large Head Start Center, I approached the large, beautiful old stucco building with excitement and anxiety.

I had just earned a master's degree in early childhood education after doing my undergraduate work and teaching for a few years in Taiwan, where I grew up. The center was anxious to hire me in the middle of the year because they had recently lost the head teacher in one of their 4-year-olds' classrooms. This was my chance to reach out to the children I care so much about and use my creativity in new ways.

My class of 20 children was all African American, as were the other teachers at the center. I was somewhat self-conscious because of the racial and cultural differences, especially since I was still working hard on my accent and trying to fit in. I knew that one challenge I would face immediately was learning as much as I could about the culture and lives of my children. I was confident, however, in my teaching abilities and my commitment to child-centered learning.

After a few weeks it became clear to me that the transition wasn't going to be as smooth as I expected. I felt like an outsider. The other teachers, including Shawanda, the assistant teacher in my room, had all worked at the center for years. They had established their own way of doing things, and they made it clear that they didn't want me to change anything.

I could understand how they felt. Who was I, this young woman full of new ideas, to tell them how to manage the classroom? Everything had been just fine (at least to them) before I came, and they had little understanding of what I wanted to do.

Each morning, for example, the children ate breakfast when they came in, then lined up to brush their teeth and use the bathroom. Shawanda was in charge of this routine, and she insisted that the children line up quietly to await their turns. The bathroom holds only three at a time. Not surprisingly, the children found ways to entertain themselves while waiting in line—ways that Shawanda did not approve of. Each morning I cringed as she yelled at the kids to stand still and wait their turns. I finally decided this had to change, and I worked out a way for the children to use the bathroom in small groups, taking turns while the rest of the class did activities at the tables.

The center uses the High/Scope curriculum model, with which I am very comfortable. I had planned many hands-on science, art, and sensory activities. Shawanda leads one of our groups during small-group, planning, and review times, and she just couldn't understand why we were doing these types of activities. I kept wondering to myself, What were the children doing before I came?

Shawanda let me know her feelings in words and actions—I often found myself supervising the whole class while she sullenly swept the floor or wiped the tables. She complained about my lesson plans and occasionally brought up the fact that she thought the children had trouble understanding me because of my accent. I was gradually losing my self-confidence.

The other major conflict was how we handled misbehavior. We had a few children who brought a lot of anger and stress to school. They often lost control and became aggressive and violent. My preferred approach was to separate them from the rest of the group, talking quietly to them and teaching them ways to control their anger. I thought it was critical to preserve their sense of self and not add to their anger and frustration.

Shawanda, on the other hand, resorted to punishment. She missed the time-out chair, which I had done away with, and I often heard her threatening the children with telling their parents or taking away privileges, or simply yelling at them to induce humiliation.

Meanwhile the director gave me positive feedback. She told me she was thrilled with the level of creativity I had brought to the classroom, encouraging the children to use their imaginations in many ways. She also understood what I was going through with Shawanda. She respected the knowledge that Shawanda had gained from so many years of teaching, but she admitted that the teaching assistants needed a better understanding of developmentally appropriate practice. She was working hard on a professional development program.

The end of the school year is in sight. Our center closes for two months, and my director has asked me for a commitment to teach the same class next year. But every time I think about how difficult my job is trying to work with Shawanda, I do not know whether to stay or look elsewhere.

Will Shawanda eventually understand and embrace my philosophy and goals, or am I fighting a losing battle?

Discussion questions

1. Retell this case from Shawanda's point of view. Why do you think that Shek-yee and Shawanda have such different viewpoints?

2. What advice would you give Shek-yee about working with Shawanda? What actions could they take to improve their working relationship? What is the director's role in helping to improve this relationship?

3. Have you ever had conflicts with other staff members or people you have worked with? Compare the sources of tension you have experienced to those of others in your discussion group. What conclusions can you draw about working relationships?

4. In what specific ways can you learn more about the culture and lives of the children you work with?

5. Besides the tension between Shawanda and Shek-yee, what other issues can you identify in this case? Brainstorm as many ideas as you can.

How Can We Work Like This?

Pauline has been teaching kindergarten in an urban school for eight years. This past year her classroom was converted into two rooms so that the school could have full-day kindergarten programs. Pauline wonders how she can continue to teach under the adverse conditions this has caused.

As I try to read the children a story, the noise from the classroom next to us is making me crazy. If I'm so distracted by the noise, how can I expect the children to be able to pay attention? I struggle through the book. I think the children are glad when I tell them we will do a project at the tables.

I have taught kindergarten in this same urban public school for the last eight years. Most of the time I felt I was doing a pretty good job. Now I realize how good I really had it.

Our school district, like a few of the other large urban districts, is under state control because of mismanagement and low student achievement. As part of the court mandate, the district has been given money for all-day kindergarten programs instead of half day. The rationale of course is that putting money into early childhood programs helps the children be ready for formal schooling and not fall so far behind.

In our school, however, there was no space in which to add the two new classrooms needed for four full-day kindergarten programs. Instead of new rooms, the two existing kindergarten rooms have been converted into two classrooms each, using storage cabinets or waist-high dividers to divide the rooms. Nothing else changed. So now 52 children and 4 teachers occupy the spaces that held 26 children and 2 teachers last year.

The children at our school are tough kids. They have many stressful aspects to their lives, and for many of them school is a place to calm down and relax. I find that with the children in such tight quarters, there are many more behavior problems than before. The children always seem to be pushing and tripping each other, causing a high degree of frustration. And to top it off, the children now get to spend *all day* instead of half the day cramped in this room.

We have always had difficulty getting basic supplies, so I had gotten good at begging and borrowing art materials, math manipulatives, and storage containers. But now I hardly ever get to use those things. It is almost impossible to have activity centers because there's no room beyond the tables where the children sit. And with two classes of children, the noise level can become unbearable. I also feel like I am constantly tripping over Mary, my assistant teacher.

I know the children need to get up and move around, but the only activities easily managed in our space are group activities with the children at the tables. I feel as though I am compromising tremendously on what I know is best for the children. How can I give them the best possible experiences under these conditions?

Discussion questions

1. Brainstorm all the possible ways that the physical environment can affect children's behavior.

2. What advice do you have for Pauline? What suggestions do you have for her use of the cramped space? What suggestions do you have for the problem of the noise level between the two classes?

3. If you were to speak at the district board of education meeting, what would you say to convince the board to increase the space allotted to kindergarten?

4. Do you believe that full-day kindergarten is more beneficial than half day? Justify your position with specific reasons.

5. What other examples have you come across of teachers working under adverse conditions? How have they coped?

Questioning the Principal

Veronica takes a child who has hit her to the principal's office to be disciplined. Instead, the principal reprimands Veronica for the way she grabbed the child. Veronica feels that she is being treated unprofessionally and will have difficulty in her relationships with the child and the principal as a result.

Tonight is Fall Fun Night at our school. This means, of course, that the kids have been distracted for days by the anticipation of wearing their costumes and playing games. I feel like I've been losing control all week.

This is my second year of teaching, so I'm still working hard on my classroom management skills. My biggest problem is Andrew. He is the only child who constantly challenges me. He talks back, he calls out, and he has yet to get his work done on time. I would say that 90 percent of the time Andrew acts inappropriately, even for a first-grader. He can't work with a partner without one of them ending up in tears. He often resorts to hitting or kicking when he is frustrated. I was determined that today, even if I did nothing else, I would at least exercise some management and have order.

The bell rang and the children came in and put away their things. They started to get crazy, but I quickly nipped that in the bud by organizing some enjoyable projects I had planned. The class was amazingly good and productive. We even got to do some fun activities because the children were working so well. All except Andrew. He ended up not being allowed to participate because he would not share the materials on the table. He spent the time working alone in his seat.

At lunchtime I called everyone to get in line and get ready to walk down the hall. The children know that there is no talking in the hall because other classes are working. I sometimes let them whisper to passing teachers or friends, but they must not use loud voices ever. Well, as we lined up, Andrew kicked the child in front of him. I warned him calmly that he needed to keep his hands and feet to himself or he would be moved to the end of the line. Next he began yelling at the people in the hall walking past our door. I told him that he was the only one who was having trouble controlling his mouth and his body. I turned around to get ready to go when I heard *snap!* Andrew had let the rabbit out of its cage and it was running around the classroom. I told Andrew to move to the end of the line, then I scooped up the rabbit and put it back in its cage.

The children moved out of the classroom and down the hall. By now Andrew was again kicking the child in front of him. I took him by the arm and walked right next to him. Instead of cooperating he turned around and smacked me hard on my arm.

I was shocked. I had never before been hit by a child, and I couldn't believe it. I grabbed Andrew by the arm and pulled him aside. I explained in my sternest voice that this was not acceptable behavior. One of the other teachers in the hall came over and told me that I should report Andrew to the principal immediately. She walked my class down to the lunchroom.

By the time I got to Mrs. Carlan's office, Andrew was in tears. With Andrew listening I tried to explain to her the details of the incident in a way in which he couldn't interrupt. To my dismay, as I was explaining what had happened, Mrs. Carlan reprimanded me

Giving It Some Thought

in front of Andrew. She said, "You should never touch a student. You have no reason to ever touch one of the children here like that."

I was furious. Even if I were wrong and had inappropriately touched a child, I should not have been reprimanded in front of him. Mrs. Carlan could have sent Andrew back to class and spoken to me in private. And on top of that, Andrew did not even get admonished. He got away with hitting a teacher!

I don't know how I will exercise authority over Andrew now. And I don't know what kind of relationship I will have with the principal!

Discussion questions

1. What do you consider the major issues in this case? Brainstorm as many as you can. Which are the most important ones? Why?

2. What have you learned about classroom management that could help Veronica?

3. What suggestions do you have for changing Andrew's behavior?

4. How do you feel about the principal's reaction to the incident? Do you think she acted unprofessionally? Why or why not?

5. What do you think Veronica can do to improve her relationship with Mrs. Carlan? With Andrew?

Strike!

Danielle is a kindergarten teacher in a school district that is about to go on strike. As a nontenured teacher she is struggling with whether to participate in the strike. Danielle also wonders what effect the current job action is having on her children.

We all left the meeting keyed up. The strike date was set for two weeks from today. Our building strike captains spent the meeting time laying out plans for picket lines and the other procedures, should it come to a strike.

When I started my teaching career last year, I never thought that I would be preparing to strike. I feel as if I am coasting on a wave that is taking me crashing into shore. I don't know what to expect, and some days I really feel I am in over my head.

The strike has been coming for a long time. Our school district's management has been under state control for many years, like that of many of the urban districts in our state. We have been working without a contract for almost two years. Since the state takeover we have been subjected to unannounced supervisory visits to check that we are exactly on the right lesson plan at the right moment. The visitors have been nicknamed "SWAT teams," and sometimes I feel like we are indeed engaged in battle. Most of my colleagues think the union's actions are necessary because we are not treated like professionals. We are not allowed to make professional decisions about curriculum, assessment, time management, and so on.

We are already participating in a job action in which we do only what was stipulated in our previous contract. This includes being in the school only during the hours outlined in the contract. We

Giving It Some Thought

arrive 15 minutes before the children, and we leave 15 minutes after they do. Teachers refuse to conduct any of the special after-school programs, we have no bulletin board displays or children's art hanging in the hallways, and we proudly wear our Settle Now! buttons on our coats.

The strict hours are a problem for me because I need extra time in school to finish my work—to get a handle on the mounds of paperwork required, put my plan book in order for my supervisor, and prepare teaching materials and activities. My kids asked me if they could hang their artwork in the hallway, as they used to do, and I've told them that we can't do it right now. Maybe I owe them more of an explanation. I feel that this job action hurts my teaching and in the short run also hurts the experience my kids get at school.

The strike possibility also poses a dilemma for me. I am teaching kindergarten for only my second year. That means I am not tenured, and I worry about my job security. The union representatives repeatedly tell the nontenured faculty not to worry because the union will take legal action to support anyone who is fired due to the work action or the strike. That's asking me to put a lot of trust in a union I've only been a member of for a year and a half.

What will I do if we actually go out on strike? The union is very powerful, as are most unions in this county, so I feel that I can't possibly go against the strike and report for work. However, I don't want to lose my job either. And I'm worried about what will happen to my kids if I don't come in to work.

What should I do?

Discussion questions

1. What issues should Danielle consider in making a decision about whether to participate in the strike or not? How many issues can you identify?

2. If you were in Danielle's position, how would you explain your decision to the children in your class? To the parents?

3. If Danielle decides to honor the strike, what effect might the temporary change in teacher and routine have on the children?

4. Do you believe teachers should be unionized? Why or why not?

5. New teachers become socialized into the school's culture. The union is only one of the socializing factors. What other factors can you identify?

The Teachers' Room

Sandra is frustrated by the negative attitude of many of the teachers in the urban public school where she has begun teaching. In this climate she wonders how she will keep alive her desire to teach.

I was thrilled to begin my first teaching job at Lincoln Elementary School in the heart of one of the poorest neighborhoods in the city where I grew up. Although the surrounding neighborhood looked like a war zone, the inside of Lincoln was bright and full of the promise of young children. At least to me it was. I got the job teaching second grade in October, when another teacher left the school.

I was assigned a mentor, Karen, to help me through my first year. Having a mentor is part of the state-required induction program for new teachers. Karen was eager to introduce me to her co-workers, and I met a few teachers as I came in the first day. During my planning period Karen walked with me to the teachers' room. We ran into the reading specialist in the hallway. She seemed very friendly, but as the three of us walked down the hall, I began to feel a little uncomfortable.

The two teachers pointed out a little girl standing in the hallway. She looked nervous. "Oh, that child's a head case," the reading specialist said before I even had a chance to ask about her. She added, "She likes to wait to see if her teacher is in the classroom before she goes in with the rest of her classmates, and she gets upset and cries whenever she has trouble reading." I personally saw nothing unusual about this and certainly no reason to put down the child in front of me. I felt that they were acting unprofessionally and should have shown more respect for the child.

Giving It Some Thought

As the weeks went by, I began to wonder if I was the only person in the school with a positive outlook toward the children. Sitting in the teachers' room for lunch, I have listened quietly to the horrible things the teachers say about the children. Many of the stories make me believe that the individual children could be helped if only the teachers would take the time and make the effort.

It's January, and Karen has already given up on two of her students. She says there is no way they will be promoted to third grade without a miracle. If you know a child is falling behind, I think you should take extra time to help him. I understand that some children just can't grasp some things, but isn't it our job to try our best to help them?

I think that many of the teachers here have been teaching for so long that they have gotten used to going to work uninspired, getting through the day, and collecting their paychecks. What happened to teachers who would teach interesting lessons and try to make a difference in a child's life? What has happened to my colleagues since they first began teaching? Maybe I'm being too idealistic, but these teachers are not trying their hardest. In a few years will I lose my spark, my desire to touch the life of a child, the way my co-workers have?

Discussion questions

1. What do you believe has happened to Sandra's colleagues since they began their teaching careers? Do you know teachers who have *not* lost their inspiration after years of teaching? What do you think makes the difference? What factors can you identify that lead to burnout?

2. What can beginning teachers do to prevent burnout? What professional advice would you give Sandra to keep her motivation high?

3. Do you think Sandra is being too idealistic? Can teachers make a difference with all children simply by trying harder?

4. What is the role of the leadership in the school in helping create a more positive workplace? How does the school climate affect how children learn? What about in a child care center?

5. What specific characteristics would you look for in determining the climate of a school or a child care center?

Is Teaching Really for Me?

Frances is beginning her first teaching experience and her lesson doesn't go the way she envisioned it. She feels discouraged and wonders if she is cut out to be a teacher.

On Wednesday I was to conduct my very first lesson plan for Mrs. Harman's first-grade class. I had been visiting the class one day each week for the past month. It was my first teaching practicum, although I was taking my second course in the teacher preparation program at the college. I was looking forward to planning a lesson and taking over the class.

Mrs. Harman asked me to plan something for their math period. The children had been learning about counting by ones and by tens, so I needed to come up with an activity that would incorporate these skills. I thought it would be useful if the children created their own math manipulatives following pictures they had seen in their workbooks—kidney beans glued on Popsicle sticks. I would bring in a mystery bag full of beans and have the children guess what they would be working with.

Before class started I told Mrs. Harman, "I am so nervous. I really don't know how to conduct this lesson and I have no idea how to begin or what to say."

Mrs. Harman tried to help me relax, saying, "You'll be okay. And I will be here to help you out."

Well, math period came too soon, and before I knew it I was sitting in the Author's Chair with 25 children in front of me. I began by asking, "Who can count by tens?" The children began calling out, "10, 20, 30, . . . ". Then I said, "We are going to do an activity using familiar objects to count out tens and ones. But first you have to guess what the objects are in the mystery bag!" I held up the bag for everyone to see.

Many hands went up excitedly and I pointed to Irene, a child I was familiar with. Irene answered, "Beans!"

Great. Now what was I going to do? I thought this part would take more time and build up motivation for the lesson by eliciting many different guesses.

"Does anyone else want to try to guess?" I asked, hoping we could stretch this a little further. Everyone else that I called on agreed with Irene. I didn't know what else to say. I hadn't planned on their guessing beans right away.

I showed the children the beans inside the bag and asked them where they had seen beans on Popsicle sticks. Without hesitation they said in their math books. I asked, "Wouldn't it be cool to make real counting sticks with these beans?" "Yeah!" they answered.

I asked Mrs. Harman to pair up the children and sit them at the tables. I realized it would be more instructive to give each pair a different number of beans to count out for their Popsicle sticks. So I walked around the room, individually giving each set of partners a number. This confused the children a bit. Also, I had no plan for where they were going to put the leftover beans after they had glued the tens on the stick.

It took the kids all of five minutes to complete the assignment. Including the guessing and the directions, only about 15 minutes had passed. I still had 45 minutes to teach math. The children started growing restless and impatient. Mrs. Harman saw my discomfort and immediately jumped in, having the children get out their workbooks and turn to one of the lessons that uses the bean counting sticks.

I realized I had not been adequately prepared to teach this lesson. In fact, I began to wonder if I was cut out for teaching at all. Shouldn't this stuff come naturally? I felt as though I had no idea how to speak to the children, how to give them directions, and I definitely had no concept of time. I felt badly that Mrs. Harman had had to bail me out, although she was very kind and understanding. I left school that day wondering if I had the knack for teaching.

Discussion questions

1. Do you think that teaching takes a special knack, or can good teaching be learned? How much of teaching is an art? A science?

2. If possible, interview some experienced teachers. Did they struggle to learn how to teach in the beginning, or did they feel it came naturally to them?

3. What advice would you give Frances for preparing her next lesson for the children? What specific suggestions can you make?

4. What developmental characteristics of first-graders does Frances need to keep in mind when planning lessons?

5. What do you think the role of the mentor teacher should be? How much should the mentor take over? How much should she step back and let the student teacher learn from her mistakes? What has been your own experience?

Resources for further reading

Baptiste, N. 1995. Resources for understanding who you work with in your early childhood setting. *Early Childhood Education Journal* 23 (2): 111–13.
    This article focuses on the idea that the quality of adult-adult interactions is critical to high-quality programs. Resources are offered to help adults learn more about adult development and individual differences among co-workers.

Baptiste, N., & M. Sheerer. 1997. Negotiating the challenges of the "survival" stage of professional development. *Early Childhood Education Journal* 24 (4): 265–67.
    This article highlights the frustration that first-year teachers and directors may suffer if they don't have the support system they need. Suggestions are given for the positive use of mentors in professional development.

Chenfeld, M.B. 1993. *Teaching in the key of life.* Washington, DC: NAEYC.
    This inspirational book includes a series of essays that help teachers think deeply about what it feels like to be children in early childhood classrooms. Chenfeld's reflections and anecdotes will remind teachers about why they wanted to become teachers in the first place.

Covey, S.R. 1989. *The seven habits of highly effective people: Restoring the character ethic.* New York: Simon & Schuster.
    In this best-selling trade book, Covey outlines seven habits intended to help readers find personal integrity and build positive relationships. Through anecdotes and reflections, the book offers insights on how "character ethic" can lead to fulfillment in one's personal and professional life.

Feeney, S., & N.K. Freeman. 1999. *Ethics and the early childhood educator: Using the NAEYC code.* Washington, DC: NAEYC.

This book, like the NAEYC Code of Ethical Conduct, seeks to inform, not prescribe, answers to tough decisions that teachers face as they work with children and families. Well-chosen examples and questions clarify key points about ethical conduct and decisionmaking, stimulating reflection and discussion on critical issues that confront us all.

Feeney, S., & K. Kipnis. 1997. *Code of ethical conduct and statement of commitment. Guidelines for responsible behavior in early childhood education*. Washington, DC: NAEYC.

Revised in 1997, this booklet offers guidelines for responsible behavior and sets forth a common basis for resolving ethical dilemmas in early childhood care and education. It lists both ideals and principles regarding ethical responsibilities to children, families, and colleagues and to the community and society.

Jones, E., ed. 1993. *Growing teachers: Partnerships in staff development*. Washington, DC: NAEYC.

This collection of true stories describes some of the challenges that early childhood teachers face and the way that mentors help them grow professionally. In a positive, motivational way, this book presents views of what is possible in staff development.

NAEYC. 1994. Position statement: A conceptual framework for early childhood professional development. *Young Children* 49 (3): 68–77.

This position statement identifies the diverse roles and settings within the field of early childhood education. It defines six levels of professional development based on educational preparation and outlines a unifying framework for a professional career lattice.

Stevens, K. 1995. Integrating new personnel: The art of building (and rebuilding) staff unity. *Child Care Information Exchange* (102): 63–68.

This article explores the role of friendship in staff relationships and describes 11 strategies for promoting positive employee relationships, especially in helping new staff and existing staff acclimate and adjust to each other.

Tertell, E.A., S.M. Klein, & J.L. Jewett, eds. 1998. *When teachers reflect: Journeys toward effective, inclusive practice*. Washington, DC: NAEYC.

By focusing on the themes of guidance, play, individualizing, collaboration, inclusion, emergent curriculum, and working with families, 18 teachers, along with their mentors, share the stories of their journeys toward more inclusive, developmentally appropriate practice.

Weiner, L. 1999. *Urban teaching: The essentials*. New York: Teachers College Press.

For teachers frustrated by the challenges of urban teaching—from overcrowded classrooms to cultural diversity—this book provides "insider" advice to help them move beyond mere survival to being effective in urban schools. Included are chapters on the urban school setting; relations with teachers, the union, and administrators; urban students; and managing the urban classroom.

Information about NAEYC

NAEYC is . . .

an organization of nearly 102,000 members founded in 1926 and committed to fostering the growth and development of children from birth through age 8. Membership is open to all who share a desire to serve young children and act on behalf of the needs and rights of all children.

NAEYC provides . . .

educational services and resources to adults and programs working with and for children, including

• *Young Children, the* peer-reviewed journal for early childhood educators

• **Books, posters, brochures, and videos** to expand your knowledge and commitment to and support your work with young children and families, including topics on infants, curriculum, research, discipline, teacher education, and parent involvement

• **An Annual Conference** that brings people together from across the United States and other countries to share their expertise and advocate on behalf of children and families

• **Week of the Young Child** celebrations sponsored by more than 400 NAEYC Affiliate Groups to call public attention to the critical significance of the child's early years

• **Insurance plans** for members and programs

• **Public affairs information** and access to information through NAEYC resources and communication systems for conducting knowledgeable advocacy efforts at all levels of government and through the media

• **A voluntary accreditation system** for high-quality programs for children through the National Academy of Early Childhood Programs

• **Resources and services** through the National Institute for Early Childhood Professional Development, working to improve the quality and consistency of early childhood preparation and professional development opportunities

• **Young Children International** to promote international communication and information exchanges

For information about membership, publications, or other NAEYC services, visit NAEYC online at **www.naeyc.org**

National Association for the Education of Young Children
1509 16th Street, NW, Washington, DC 20036-1426
202-232-8777 or 800-424-2460